M000195109

The Normal Side of Insanity

Marynell Lund

INFINITY
PUBLISHING

All rights reserved. No part of this book shall be reproduced or transmitted in any form or by any means, electronic, mechanical, magnetic, photographic including photocopying, recording or by any information storage and retrieval system, without prior written permission of the publisher. No patent liability is assumed with respect to the use of the information contained herein. Although every precaution has been taken in the preparation of this book, the publisher and author assume no responsibility for errors or omissions. Neither is any liability assumed for damages resulting from the use of the information contained herein.

Copyright © 2010 by Marynell Lund

ISBN 0-7414-5896-9

Printed in the United States of America

Published March 2010

INFINITY PUBLISHING
1094 New DeHaven Street, Suite 100
West Conshohocken, PA 19428-2713
Toll-free (877) BUY BOOK
Local Phone (610) 941-9999
Fax (610) 941-9959
Info@buybooksontheweb.com
www.buybooksontheweb.com

Contents

Acknowledgments

This book is dedicated to my friend Beth that bestowed love upon me. She took the time to say a kind word or give a pat on the back. Beth listened while I poured out my heart and crawled through the darkness of myself to find an inner peace within.

Beth stood strong while I felt weak and defeated. Through my eyes and looking into hers, I saw her look back at me with acceptance. You Beth, and you alone, guided me through my own hell and were still there at the end. I dedicate this book to you Beth Daniels, may God continue to bless you.

Thanks also to Kathy Bassett for her ability to capture my pain in her illustration for my book. I will be forever grateful. Kathy you were there to give me a push and helpful advice which helped me to keep my direction. Edith Branstrom you were always there too and I would not be alive today if you had not stopped me. God Bless you as you have so richly blessed my life. Thank you to Marilyn Morrison for helping with the "nuts and bolts" and layout for my book. Without you I would still be looking at blank pages.

Psalms 27, Verse 10:

"For my father and my mother have forsaken me, but the Lord will take me up.

In the midst of mothers and daughters, there are only survivors, survivors with or without success. Can one ever understand why the pain and torture, why the battle lines, when neither asked to be born but both asked to survive? Some survive by denial while others survive by reality. Either way the price for survival is high, sometimes too high. I paid a high price for survival. Feel blessed if none of this makes sense to you for then you can feel that what you had or have as a mother or daughter must be better than what you will read. Remember too that with each passing we leave a print on each person we encounter. If your print does not matter to you then chances are you will leave a print of pain but if by chance you care then the print you leave may be that of a blessing. If people worked as hard at being kind as they do at being cruel, the heart would bleed less, ache less, and bruise less. You will feel and live my pain and you will search in the depths of your mind what you think the answers to unanswered questions should have been but in the end you too will find that there are gray areas but with God as your guide you can learn to live with an outcome and mold an inner peace that most do not find. Money will not buy inner peace. I feel lucky as most go through life not knowing why they were born or what they were meant to do instead of living life spiritually and thankfully. I have this inner peace and know why I am alive and how to live and love. No one in the end took anything from me. You are only a loser if you so choose to be a loser.

At birth you receive a name and a certificate of who you are, whom you belong to, and no instructions on how to raise the child. When you think of it, it is funny because when you buy a lawn mower or other product to use it comes with instructions on how to use or work the item. When my first born was laid in my arms I did not have a clue as to what a mother is so I took all the good qualities from the aunts that I loved and tried to treat my children like they did me. I also treated my children like I wished I would have been treated.

When you are given a child, it is assumed that everyone knows the rules and the outcome. Whatever happens in between is subject to interpretation by outsiders after the fact. What if, just what if the child is given to a mother incapable of loving! The mother than places that child at the mercy of others, who then pays for the sin? Who then do the children become?

Having children after having been through all this as a child, I should have been an abuser myself. I should have had no parenting skills of a positive nature or the ability to love unconditionally after all I had experienced.

No Going Back

Never had I gone back down "memory lane" as they say. What in the world was memory lane suppose to be anyway? Lane? It was down a dusty gravel road with too much gravel centered on the road and if you didn't drive according to the conditions you could easily find yourself in the ditch, I know as I almost went in several times. There use to be a thick grove that connected to the driveway like a solid wall of green on each side and the floor of the grove was covered in lily of the valley and the smell would take your breath away and if that didn't then it was the lilacs that closed in the west side of the lawn.

Now as I drive up the driveway the south side was bare and lay in plowed ground, the old tree that held our swing was gone. The old garage where we showered was gone. The home place stood on display for all to see as they drove by. When I was a child, the house lay hidden in the vast groves of trees that surrounded our property. Off in the distance I could see the old home that my grandparents lived in with all nine children. My grandparents are only a 5x7 picture to me as they were both gone before I was born and yet I felt their life run through me, their traits among the many I have. Their presence was always in that house, as the interior of the house had not changed at all through the years other than the patterns of wallpaper on the walls and the patterns of linoleum on the floors.

Upon entering the kitchen, I had visions of how the kitchen sink use to be cluttered with mom's collection of makeup and wind song perfume. Even now it is as if the perfume lingers in the air and runs a chill over me. Could she be here still watching, lingering, and wanting to jump out at me one more time? Lined in the window ledge just above the kitchen sink stood a long line of medication and mostly narcotic. Mom took tranquilizers, diet pills, and sleeping pills. She loved those bottles and I hated those bottles as they took her away from me and made her feel cold and clammy. They made her feel warm and alive but only to her. I don't want to touch you as you are so cold. I had to stay alert to stay alive and she lived for staying dull and numb and lifeless. What was so good about feeling nothing, knowing nothing, and sharing nothing? I shudder at the thought that she still has an invisible hand on me. That is why I am here to confront my fears, confront the inner child in me, and separate myself from the pain of what use to be.

The cistern pump stood on the right side of the sink and the rust lay testament to the many times the handle had pumped the rusty water. It looked as though that priming the pump would be an all day job knowing the leathers have stood dry for so long and I am not sure that it had any more pumps to give. The handle stood half way up and half way down. Life was half way up and half way down. The cold metal of the pump had served many a glass of water to settle a thirst from hard work or down a hand full of pills. Everything has a purpose and a place. No more would the pump have to be primed or serve anyone. Time marches on as the testament of the leathers scream out for priming. Wouldn't it be nice if we could all be primed? Perhaps that is why I am here to get re-primed for a smoother life.

The old trash burner still stood in the same spot as it had since I can remember; not quite in the center of the kitchen floor but close enough to the center. The old stove pipes still connected as I gazed up to them it triggered the memory of my bird, Skippy, my great aunt Inez Keeler had given me. 'Oh no Skippy!" He had gotten away from me and mom was screaming, "Nanell get that damn bird away from me oh shit here it comes, get it away from me right now." If mom goes nuts now it will surely be my fault. Poor Skippy landed on top of the stovepipe burning his claws, landing on the floor trying to hold his claws up, and sticking his wings out to try to balance him. He survived all this but not without going through having his claws wrapped up and losing the ends of them. Funny how the same stovepipe was still there and funny that I even remembered it. There were so many out bursts that would have been seen as cruel but it was an everyday occurrence.

Next is the dining room and living room, these two rooms opened into one big room with the other end being the living room area. Mom and dad's bedroom was to the right past the oil burner. The pattern on the linoleum was rubbed smooth from the bedroom through into the kitchen. Perhaps this showed the many steps that my dad took every morning to bring mom coffee in bed and refills as well. The many steps dad walked to try and keep peace. The stand by the bed was still there with cigarette ashes and cigarette butts running over the edges of the ashtray. Bright red lipstick still clung to the filters. Again my skin crawled, I spun around. Oh gosh it was as if she should be there yelling, "Nanell clean that ashtray up for mama and wipe the top of the stand. You get the hell out of the house and do not come in until I say you can, you hear me?"

When the house was alive with a family inside, all you needed to do is close your eyes and you could smell the strong perfume of mom and the velvet tobacco that dad smoked in his pipe. To me, the pipe smelled much better than the strong odor of perfume.

In the dining room was a built in cubby hole that had once been a see through into the pantry of the house, which later became our indoor bathroom. I was twelve years old when we got our first bathroom. My great uncle and great aunt had bought all the necessary bathroom fixtures, plumbing needs, and my dad and great uncle turned the pantry into a bathroom. I would not have to make anymore-barefoot trips to the outhouse. No more running as fast as my feet could carry me because I just knew there was a bear about to reach out and grab me. No more of that but then

3

there are tradeoffs. I could actually lock the door and get naked but I always kept my eye on the door knob watching for it to move. There is no time to relax after having been molested; sometimes it hurts so bad to set my naked bottom down; always feeling bruised and sore. A soreness that I thought was visible for all to see. My bottom had that full aching feeling as I stood here thinking about the private bath that never felt private.

In the dead of winter when the plumbing would freeze up, we would have to use a "honey bucket" which was nothing more than a milk pail with handle hinges that dug into you no matter how you straddled it. The bucket stood in the center of the bathroom floor cold and stinking to high heaven. Still it was better than running outside and most times not being able to get to far away from the house to do our business! In the night I just knew something or someone was out to get me. Even now when I think about it, it still makes my ears ring and heart pound. I hate this feeling as I need to have my keenest edge to deal with what may be coming and all I hear is my inner fear surging through my heart and ears.

Before we had the bathroom, we took showers out in an old out building with a homemade shower, which was nothing more than being able to stand on two, two by eight boards for the floor of the shower. The shower floor stood upon black silt dirt. A large sprinkler can tied to an old piece of water hose was wrapped around the rafter above our head and twine string handle was tied to the can so all we had to do was pull that twine string rope and tip the can down with cool water. The shower water was hauled out there usually be 10:00 in the morning with the hopes that the afternoon sun would shine in and warm the water up.

The front doors to the shed lay propped up with wooden fence post at a slant so no one could see you directly but with a little turning and straining, one could easily see you. The shower ended fighting off mosquitoes and landing mud splatters on your legs and having muddy toes to get out of their and run back to the house. All you had to do was sit on

4

the sidewalk step in the summer and the heat from the step would take the chill off your feet and help dry the mud spatters.

In the winter, my bathtub was to have water pumped in the big kitchen sink and dad would heat water with a teakettle and pour scalding hot water in to warm it up. Dad would sit with his back to me at the kitchen table and play solitaire all the while I kept one eye on him and one eye on the kitchen door as we never had any locks on any of our doors. In those days, no one locked his or her doors. I always feared that my brother or uncle Lewis would walk in on me. Always fear so much fear that I do not remember any comfort or childhood laughter only fear of the known actions of man and the actions of a crazy mother.

You can bet your bottom dollar that my mom never set foot in no dirt floor garage and showered, why she would not be caught dead doing that. We all had to stay out of the house so she could have the entire privacy of the kitchen for her. In the summer the east kitchen window stood open ajar and we always knew when she was done with her shower as the wind song perfume escaped through the window and no matter where we were outside the stench of that perfume would find my nostrils every time.

We never once owned a washer or dryer. Our basement could not house them, as that was just a dirt cellar with only one tiny light bulb to light up the dingy basement. We always hauled the laundry to town and if it were too bad for too long then I would wash clothes out in the kitchen sink and drape them over chairs and the doors to the oil burner that stood in the living room. It was all too common to walk through the house and step in little puddles of water from the drippings of the wet clothes.

The upstairs in the house consisted of creaking steps on the third, eighth and top step. If you spread your feet wide apart as you sailed up the steps you could avoid the noise, which you wanted to do at all costs. To wake either mom or dad would be hell on wheels, especially mom. If mom were home, she would yell and scream at you to get back in bed, never mind you had to pee and if you woke dad up, he just might end up coming upstairs. A part of my life's lesson was to learn the steps but I kept it to myself and I managed to work my way around.

My sleeping quarters were mostly under the bed or in the back of my tiny closet hidden behind a burned out vacuum cleaner in the corner. My back was to the wall and straining through the night shadows to watch for dad to come into my room. He did not know or did not have his mind on the creak in the steps but I heard them and I always knew how close he was.

Now as I stand in front of the closet door and peering into the room the faint smell of my dad is ever present. Look now dad do you see the scared helpless child hiding in the back only wanting you to leave and then we could be OK? As I look into the closet now my heart bleeds for the child that is no longer hidden there out of fear. Where did the child go, I want to hold you so that you never hurt again. Oh your sad little face, come on honey I will hold you. What an outer body experience to see me as that small child huddled and scared in the back of the closet. I silently stood there curling my arms together and digging into my arms in a tight hug. You poor baby why did this have to happen to you, why did they hurt you? Suddenly the tears blurred my eyes so that I could no longer tell what I was seeing but I knew what I was feeling. I had never known such sorrow as I did at this moment of confronting my inner child. Go ahead and cry it is all over now. No longer will my inner child hurt. What was there left to work with? How do you say good-bye to yourself, your childhood? No longer do you exist.

Maybe life was not as it should be in my eyes or God's eyes but it was my life. For me to take anything good from my life I must take these stories and build on them, and on the laughter, and quaint things that I know see. Is it more wise to judge or to let others judge? I have pondered this all my life. If I hate any of my life then I have to hate myself as all of this life good or bad is what made me, me. From the outside, the answers always appear simple and in black and white but when it is you in my shoes then you will find that where you step sometimes is also in a gray area. If only a portion is evil but all else is good then does the good wipe out the evil? Is all-good lost because of a portion of evil? All these questions will be answered or are answered in time. Do the answers really matter? There is much to ponder in life while life is going on all around you.

My memories have never been lost only cluttered as if they were strewn all over a desk and as I pick up each memory I am once again flooded with the task at hand as to what to do with it. I do not dwell on that, as I believe that God wanted me to share and to reflect by taking you down to the depths of my core being and come back up with me to realize that you can be all right. This does not mean that you will be all right every day of your life but overall, you can make a life and you can be all right. Life is nothing more than steps and some days we take many steps and other days we may step backwards but now as an adult we must take those steps for our self and by our self but do remember that God is with us each step of the way.

We all have our own way of filing our segments of life. Some choose to bury them in the shoebox of their soul for safekeeping and I understand that. My time to share and write is for me like the calm after the storm. The washing in of the tide, and now the tide of yesterday flows out to sea to never more be repeated.

My Role Models

Dad

Dad was 42 years old when I was born. He would start his days with coffee, and playing cards to limber up his hands before going out to milk. The morning would be full of his noises which consisted of him banging his pipe on the edge of the trash burner to begin the morning with a fresh pull of tobacco, then there would be his morning coughing to free up his lungs of yesterdays smoke to make room for some more. In the wintertime he would spend the early morning hours stoking up the trash burner. The house smelled of burning corncobs and apple wood blended in with various other pieces of wood, and the smell of his velvet tobacco pipe. If the damper is not adjusted just right then the strong smell of smoke traveled through the house to find a different route to escape.

My morning wake up call for school would be dad opening the stair door and Pooty, my dog would trip and slip and clumsily run up the stairs to meet me and whine as if he had not seen me in years. Now that was how real love should feel like that of a puppy. "Dad I am up and getting dressed." I would yell this to keep him from using the excuse that he had to come up and wake me up. "OK, see you after school. Try and keep warm it is a cold one out there."

No sooner would I get downstairs then mom would start in, "Nanell you better get going I hear the bus. You better not miss the bus because if you do I will not drive you to school." "Ma the bus doesn't come for twenty minutes yet." By the time I got a bowl of cereal half ate she would be yelling again. "Get your ass down to the bus I hear it coming." Many a cold mornings, I was forced out of the house only to stand at the end of the road with cold north wind whirling glistening snow pebbles around my face. The dead silence all around told me that the bus was nowhere near our place as you could hear it two miles away as it would roar to a stop and then roar off again picking up the next child for school. My hands would be aching and burning and itching from having been so cold. I could no longer feel my toes at the end of my boots.

Dad would do the morning chores and turn the cows lose in the cow yard before he would come in and eat. He always said that a man should not eat before his animals have been fed and I do not believe he ever did eat ahead of them. The cows and the milk they gave was the glue that held the old farm together and brought in the garnished milk check month after month and that same check kept the FHA at arm's length from foreclosing on our home.

We were so poor and I was always aware of this. On the farm I grew up on, not one big piece of farm machinery could be found. We had a single row corn binder that did just that went up and down one row of corn at a time and cut a batch of corn wrapped it in twine and shoved it out the back of the binder. A single row baler was used to make hay bales or straw bales. The feed grinder now stood empty and tattered from the elements of the weather. It was here that we added our own corn and oats and made our own feed for the cattle. We had a two-bottom plow. All our machinery was used and weathered from years of being stored out in the open. There was no machine shed to house the tractors. There were long hours put in on the farm from early morning until late at night, made no difference if it was spring planting time or fall harvest time. The clock still held twenty-four hours and dad worked sixteen to eighteen hours a day doing what he loved. Farming was a job that he loved and yet paid him little money.

When a much needed rain would come dad and I would go pick grub worms and angle worms so we could go down to the lake that was less than two miles from home. A catch of fresh bullheads was what dad referred to as a breakfast fit for a king. Now most would not take the time of day to fish for a bullhead, but in the spring water, the run of bullheads was a feast. Dad loved to eat fresh fish with pancakes and a batch of his homemade sauce. We cooked many meals as mom was either in the hospital or out running around. Supper was a late meal, as we had to wait until dad was done with milking before we would eat. Many times, I would eat a bowl of cereal and already be in bed as I never was one to stay up late.

When I started cooking, at the early age of five, on a chair in front of the stove there were many a burnt meal served but dad never complained and he ate it too. I know why he loved his sandwich spread. Every time we turned around the jar was empty. Now I realize that he probably ate tons of those sandwiches to fill himself up.

Life had to be very lonely for him, as mom shared no common interests with him. I often think in many ways that I, at the tender age of six, took over the role of wife, farm hand, and helper for just about anything he needed. If I was not at his side working with the animal, or working out in the field, or doing my own chore of gathering eggs and feeding chickens, then and I could be found in the house.

One particular winter we had been snowed in for quite some time and we were running low on clean clothes so I decided to do the laundry in the big single kitchen sink and started pumping the cistern handle to fetch water for heating. Looking under the kitchen sink, I did find some detergent and some Niagara flake starch. Now I thought that would be good to clean dad's thermal underwear, and socks. For some reason I thought that would make them whiter. Obviously if a little was good then a lot had to be better. I washed and I rung them out and I washed and I rinsed and by the time I did get done washing there were puddles of water at my feet from where it ran down my elbows because of having to hold my arms so high to ring out the clothing.

Running through the house and on into the living room, I would open the oil furnace door, draping the t-shirts, underwear, socks, and thermals over the doors and on top of the oil burner to get them dry by morning. When morning came, the clothes would be dry, warm and stiff as a board. I sure thought dad would think that was a nice treat especially with a cold house.

There was a twelve inch grate above the oil burner which was the only heat we had upstairs. There was little heat that flowed upward beside my bed. It was nothing to see frost an inch thick on my upstairs windows and the beautiful design in the frost to get lost in staring at it. Sometimes if the wind blew hard, there would be snow on my top cover. The windows were cracked, no storms, no screens, and the wood half rotted away from the sills. There were times in the summer I would see a bird flying around the bedroom as it had managed to sneak through the window sill ledge. One morning I woke up with a bird on my stomach! I never knew what it was like to go to sleep in a warm bedroom in the winter nor a cool bedroom in the dead of summer. Coolness in the summertime was provided by a four blade fan made of rubber that we could stop with our hands or place cards close by the turning blades and pretend that was our motorcycle.

When dad came in from milking and having dressed in the clean starched clothing, he took his shoes and socks off and began to scratch his legs as if they were on fire. "Next time try not to use so much starch honey, you did a good job but I think you need to use less starch next time OK?" It was not until years later that he shared just how broke out he was all over from head to toe.

Dad was a faithful member of the Lake Benton Legion and was up until the day he died. "You have to remember those that have gone before you and what they sacrificed for our country." Guess that had a lot to do with why I did join the Army years later. Every member would be in their uniform, participated at the ceremony at the local high school, and from there would march up to the cemetery hill, from there it would be down to the lake and the people would line up out on the pier to remember those that died at sea. A wreath would be tossed out on the lake and taps would be played and then a twenty one gun salute. From there they would bus out to the old country church with a graveside service there. The bus would bring them back to the Legion in Lake Benton where they all loved to laugh and remember the one Legion member that enjoyed his drinks maybe too much, and how he liked to stick his gun out the front door of the Legion and shoot off a round to bug the cop. When he died, all the guys leaned over each other and held their guns out the front door in salute to him. "Here is to you Donnie, by God that hurt my ears." The laughter roared and all agreed that the echo was very painful but well worth pissing the cop off in honor of Donnie. There were sobering moments, there was laughter too. This time too, was to once again share their own personal war stories and relive a part of their past that only they, as veterans, could relive it. I know now that on Memorial Day yes it is about remembering but for the remaining it is about touching base with the sacred island that they as veterans had stepped onto and would never leave until death they do part. As a child I would run over and collect the empty shell casings and use them for whistles. On the day of my dad's funeral one of the guys that had been there since I was a child, came over and handed me the empty shell casings from dad's funeral. He had remembered me collecting them as a child. On this particular day it was a bitter sweet memory.

The fundamentals of life were missing like parents parenting, religious guidance. Families that pray together stay together, I can't argue that as we are so fragmented from the point of family we are without foundation of life sustaining skills and we were never together not even in prayer. The day I was baptized was the same day dad was baptized. I only remember him going to church on my confirmation. The kids in my class called dad an old man and referred to our car as a rattrap. The backside window was missing and he had pinned up an old army green blanket and half of it flapped out the window. Kids would laugh and I remember to this day feeling embarrassed that he had come to pick me up. The kids would laugh about dad and at me when we left the house of worship. The house of worship where we were taught many different ways to be kind, reach out, and help one another. I know now they should have owned the embarrassment. Who is to say that this way of life is any better? I never made fun of them as I was too scared to open my mouth but I had a bitter heart. All of the activities that took place in the house of the Lord only added fuel to my self-perception that I did not belong here either. No one ever really seen my dad around much, some teased and called him my grandfather.

All in all dad worked all his life with no real money in hand, every season that came upon us for planting was a trip to the bank to ask for money for the crop planting. The FHA was like the big bad wolf at the door, never too far away. They wanted the buildings painted up. Truth be told with the runaway weeds that he did not have a means to cut and no extra money for repairs or paint, the farm looked in a half state of abandonment. But it still was his home place, a place that I figured he saw what he needed to see and that was no doubt the old dilapidated shack he was born in and spent his first year with all his brothers and sisters and their play area. To him, this was heaven and a familiar ground to walk upon. This farm dirt had been horse driven by his father and himself as a small boy. No FHA person could understand these things. We all have our truths and our ways of seeing things and the truth to my dad was this place was home, a home of the past, the present and he hoped the future.

I quit school in my senior year to go to work for fifty cents an hour at the local cafe up town. My dad never ever came in a restaurant but he did on this day. "What the hell are you doing here, why aren't you in school?" "I thought I could earn some money to help save the farm. Mom doesn't help you." "The farm is going to take more than you could earn here, besides your education is more important than the farm." I cried and cried for his heavy load and I wanted to take that from him. It was for sure Mom didn't give a darn. I did not like her and I did not understand why he defended her or her actions knowing all the stress she caused him.

As for the home I grew up in, it was built by my grandfather in 1910. Dad was only a year old then and he loved to tell the story of how he had to carry his own little suitcase from the old house to the new house. The old house became my house, my refuge to play in. One time I gathered up the dry leaves and small twigs and carried into the pot-bellied stove that sat there and snatched matches out to light it as I was getting cold and did not want to go in the house. Next thing I knew the smoke bellowed out the window that once held the glass to separate the outside from the inside. Dad came running from the barn, "Just what in the hell did you do?" He was worried that the old house was on fire and that I was caught in there. He was not mad at me but did take the matches away and assured me there could have been an awful fire. "It could have destroyed that house and the main house where we lived."

I got him to share some of the history of the old house and some of the items that still stood amidst the back of the fallen part of the building in its day were a dwelling for the one horse carriage. All that I could see was weathered curled up veneer shavings on the buffet that once was a testimony to its beauty

The old cook stove had a back shelf on it, which interested me. When dad started to tell me I listened with all ears and before I knew it, he had hood winked me into another one of his humorous stories. "That shelf is where I slept because there were so many kids they had no place to put me." That shelf above the cook stove was the only heat in the winter. Now you had two choices. Either you could get pissed at him for not telling you the truth to begin with, or you could laugh and get silly with him. I chose the latter.

Dad taught me how to make play out of a disaster and to find laughter through the tears of having failed at perhaps cooking something as simple as oatmeal. Now when he caught me crying over stiff oatmeal he would wrap a dishtowel around his head, get the hand eggbeater out, pour milk in, and turn the eggbeater on full speed. Imagine after a long fourteen-hour day or longer he could find it in his tired body to ease my tears and teach me to laugh at myself and he did that like fine-tuning a piano.

Many times, he made fun and laughter out of all the tasks on the farm. He had a love of the land and animals and enjoyed watching over his place and his livestock. He was not a mean man but I was afraid of him especially if he got mad. There was a quiet storm that brewed under his surface.

Mom

Mom was born and raised in Crowley La, she did not have an easy life but she did have a steady person in her life that took good care of her and was there for her. Her name was Aunt Rachel. She was the colored lady that worked for my grandmother. Grandmother was good to her and gave her a place to live and meals and they were friends.

Mom was a short, plump, black haired lady, who could charm anyone, anyone other than her immediate family. She reminded me of a cat ready to lunge, you knew she was going to but you just did not know when. She was selfish, immature, cruel, and gave little to nothing but took and even sucked your life from you if you let her. She was her happiest with a pack of Pall Mall cigarettes, a stack of quarters for the jukebox snapping her fingers and having all kinds of men lavish her with attention. She basked in the presence of others but do not expect her to give anything back at least not without motive for self-gain. Money, or sex, or clothing or even "rigged" overnight stays away from home was her haven. When I try to imagine her feeling guilty, I just do not see it. Lord knows I was busy trying to weave a childhood out of mental illness, drug addiction, incest, alcoholism, and a host of other things

The first time and the only time that I seen my grandma I was six years old. Mom and her friend Susie, and I went down to Louisiana. Upon arrival at grandma's house mom knocked on the door. Aunt Rachel answered the door with a delightful squeal and pulled us inside. She hugged mom, "Loddy Ms Mary I juz threw my corncob pipe under the bed." she said with a high pitched squeal. "Juz look at you-ins and this here young-ins why she is as pretty as a peach. Come in, come in, child you mama is right over there." With that Aunt Rachel scurried off to get us a fresh cup of cold water. I stepped from behind mom only to lay eyes on the blackest woman I had ever seen. I could not take my eyes off her. She had the whitest teeth and the prettiest smile. "Come on suga let me take you over to you-ins Granma honey. See here Ms Perkins this fine young-in Ms Mary brought along." Aunt Rachel took me over to my grandma and she hugged me tight. I was truly in awe of them. The visit was short but I still remember. Grandma and Aunt Rachel and I played old maid. I do not think I even looked at my cards once, as I could not take my eyes off Aunt Rachel. Grandma was so proud of me for drinking a tiny cup of her coffee black with no sugar or cream. That really made her proud. Mom and Susie had gone out on the town that was more important than staying with us.

When mealtime came, Aunt Rachel would sit in the stairway and eat her food and grandma would get mad and fuss at her until she would join us. She was so scared someone would just walk in and find her sitting at the table with white folk!

Grandma ran a restaurant called "Ma's Cafe" and while black people were not allowed to come inside, my grandma served anyone who wanted to eat by the back door. She did not believe in the rule and could not stand the thought of someone not being able to eat. My grandma saw no color, my mother saw no color and I was raised the same way.

Mom had never been away from her home or her mother when my dad married her and brought her up to Minnesota. Her first winter, Mom did not get out of bed. The farmhouse was cold and the only way she could stay warm was to bury herself under the covers. Dad brought her breakfast in bed every morning.

Mom always referred to the people in Minnesota as them damn yanks and how cold they {we} were as people and how nice and friendly the southern people were. She always made fun of dad's relatives and he would usually hang his head, rub his hands, and bite down on the stem of his pipe. I am sure it had to hurt his feelings as he was close to some of his sisters.

Mom dressed in the finest of outfits from matching outfit, coat, gloves, and purse. She obtained a credit card through JC Penney and charged up a bundle of money on. I remember the day the phone call came in on the charges on the card and that they needed to be paid. Dad tried to tell them they did not own a JC Penny credit card and it was not 10 minutes later mom came through the door with the largest JC Penny bag. They did not fight, dad was not a fighter but he did tell her not to charge anymore until he could get that paid off

It was perfectly fine for me to be dressed in hand me down clothes that were from a girl that was larger than me. I wore them wrinkled and saggy until mom pushed me up to an ironing board with a chair and started me out ironing my own. I did not feel pretty, I did not feel special, I did not like me, I did not like my name as some would call me Mary and I would not answer as that was my mother's name and I was not my mother. I always seen and felt her meanness as a child and on into adulthood. She was a teacher of emotional abuse. She could spurn you aside as quickly as she could entice you.

Mom never faced me when she talked to me or when I would ask her for help with schoolwork. She would be way too busy putting on her red lipstick and spray the hell out of her clothing with Wind Song perfume. Not once did she ask me how I was doing at school. She did not ask because she did not care. She did not care about the farm, the crops, the cows, the baby calves, the storm, or the drought on the crop. Mom never raised a garden not one seed was planted by her. I take that back she did scatter seeds only these were seeds of hate, deception, seeds of adultery, abuse, and neglect. All these seeds grew inside of her and produced a miserable woman. She spent her life not helping anyone else but manipulating those that stood in front of her. She did not know how to be happy for someone else or encourage someone else. All of life was at her feet to trample on as her mood saw fit to do! She gave nothing positive be it verbal or in actions.

Early on, I was her own little slave to do what she was too lazy to do. Clean and wash floors, cook meals when I was really too little to be near a hot burner. Wash clothes by hand. Do all the dishes. Oh yaw did I mention that she mainly corresponded with me by a note left on the kitchen table and she always signed it love you Nanell. Yaw she loved me but only if I got the chore list done, if not then there would be hell to pay and hollering. It did not matter if I forgot or maybe was even sick, or maybe I had stayed up past bedtime to do homework, which was always a struggle. The only real love and quiet I experienced was if I followed order and did the chores correctly.

While I have my own memories of the abuse and the fear I held for her, I learned years later that Mabel had seen the abuse but they never said or did anything because they did not know what to say or who to say it to and I get that. After all, think what an undertaking it is to report abuse. I was just grateful to have learned someone else knew about it even before I was old enough to remember it. For me, knowing Mabel knew first hand was a profound feeling of understanding.

I was thirty five years old when I decided to stand up for myself and not take any more abuse from my mother no matter what the price. This was hard to do because from the time I was a child I was told not to upset mom or she would end up in a hospital. Well she did end up in a hospital a few times and I always felt that dad blamed me. Why would I force her offer the edge and leave myself wide open for sexual abuse? It was that many years later that I had the guts to tell her what dad had done to me and all I wanted and had hoped for was a hug and her telling me she was so sorry that it had happened. Instead, what I got was her mean look and her asking me what was she supposed to do and I was not to tell anyone as others would know! There was no apology for me. She did not care what had happened to me. She did not care what this might have done to me mentally. It was at this point I learned another valuable lesson and that was to have no expectations. You do not get hurt if you have no expectations but if you do have expectations someone will ultimately let you down. Now some might think that is not a healthy outlook and maybe it isn't but it was a lot easier for me to adopt that philosophy.

Brother

By the time Dave was 15, he was already an alcoholic and I always knew how to get him in trouble if mom was home. His bedroom door would not stay open unless there was an empty paint can standing against the door holding it open. Well, when I knew he was out drinking I would close the bedroom door and stand the paint can out about 3 feet in the center of the floor and if I were a betting gal, I could have been rich, as Dave never failed to trip over the paint can. Yes! I heard the can, then I heard mom screaming at Dave, and then I would hear dad tell mom to shut up. Yes! Another small victory for me.

My brother and I did not get along and yet part of me resented him for being able to run out to our alcoholic Uncle

Lewis's trailer and get away from the hell in the house. I especially wanted him to sleep up stairs on Saturday nights, as I was so scared that a bear would come in and get me. Dave would just laugh at me and run off with Uncle Lewis.

If he played with me at all, he would play cops and robbers, I had to be the robber and go hide, and then he would go off and leave me. Playing hide and seek turned out to be the same way. Sometimes I wanted him to play dolls with me but that did not happen either. The most of what we did together was fight. He had a hell of a temper and he would get so pissed at me and would tackle me and take me down but I could always get on top of him and he could not get rid of me. When I did get up, I would run like hell for the cottonwood tree and climb as fast as my legs would carry me. Dave was afraid of heights and I knew I was safe up there but not before he would threaten me by saying, "You little son of a bitch you have to come down sometime. Sheep turd, sheep turd." He loved to call me that and he did even on the bus just to get others to laugh at me. When I think back on it, all now I cannot help but think mom is to blame for a lot of this.

Mom always pitted one against another. If she was mad at Dave and I had done a good job of cleaning she would let me know she liked me more and I remember asking her not to say that. If she was mad at me then Dave was OK. Mostly though they fought like cats and dogs too. To this day, I believe dad just plain stayed out door and stayed as busy as could be so he did not have to deal with any of it.

My brother Dave was 4 years older than I was. Dave was not happy when I showed up on the scene and that pretty much stayed true and has been true to this day. My dad shared with me on how they had brought home a new tricycle for him when I was born. They had hoped that it would ease any jealous feelings towards his new sister. On this particular morning, dad realized that Dave was being rather quiet and that was not his usual demeanor; as he walked through the house, Dave was nowhere to be found. As dad entered the bedroom, there stood Dave over the bassinet with a hammer in his hand. Dad gently took the hammer away and explained that he could have hurt me. I find this funny, as I believe that Dave knew and fully understood this was a possibility, probably one he had hoped to achieve if he had not been caught red handed.

This would not be the only time that he tried to bring a form of harm to me. Dave had been stricken with German measles and was very sick, they had told him he could not come near me, as I could get sick like him. He had kissed me in hopes of giving me the German measles. Dave replied that he thought if he kissed me, he would get rid of his measles.

As the years went by he did what he wanted to, talked back, and even told lies to get his way. He could look you right in the eye and lie to you and appeared to have no conscience. I can see now why mom and him didn't get along, it was because they were so much alike. They each had a temper, they each had addictive personalities, and they each could easily lie about what they had done or where they had been. Dad, on the other hand, was already tired and would not argue with Dave or put his foot down. I can see now that letting him run out to Lewis's trailer was an easier route then taking on Dave's bad temper. Lewis always sided with Dave and told him long ago that the door was open and that he was always welcome. How nice this was for Dave or was it! Dave had free will and all the booze he wanted. Free will may seem like a good thing as a child but free will ultimately destroyed the makings of a person, like a horse running wild with no rain to guide and direct, no boundaries

Uncle Lewis

Uncle Lewis lived on our farm in his trailer. He had never married and from the time I can remember, he drank a fifth of Old Crow every day. He was not dependable; always more in the way than anything, he too had a bad temper. He reeked of cigarettes and booze mixed with the smell of kerosene from the trailer. Dad and him farmed together and took turns with the milking, which turned out to be that dad took over on chores, as Lewis was usually drunk by evening chore time and seldom made it home on time to milk. The only thing that made this arrangement work was the fact that dad could keep a tight lid on his own temper and let things go that clearly should have been addressed.

As a child, I knew that he did not have the time of day for me unless I was going to clean his trailer for fifty cents, then he made it a point to be right there. He got a lot for the money as he would press against me, breath hard, and the smell of cigarettes and whiskey would surround me. There was no escaping him or the smell. I would get my fifty cents but not before he would feel me up and down, breathe hard, and touch me in ways that no one should touch a child.

As the years went by, he became more and more pickled and controlled by the drink. I watched him go from telling the same thing over and over and laughing at his own statements to literally squatting on the ground hugging my dog and crying his eyes out and then the rage would come or the desire to find me to touch.

Then There Was Me

Then there was me, very shy. As a child, I was the peacekeeper in the family. By that I mean if Dave and mom got into a fight it was me trying to step between them, it was me trying to get Dave to just calm down and not be so mad about everything. Then there was the job I had of keeping my mom happy and comfortable, that became the toughest chore I had and just the beginning of coming up short in her eyes. I was the one that took the abuse! Abuse I suffered from mom, dad, Dave, and Uncle Lewis. They all took from me and had a profound effect on my life. I paid a terrible price to pay for having not asked to be a part of this family. My abuse did not stop there though; I had a second cousin who also molested me. Fear and molestation was all I knew growing up but not by those words. I was systematically robbed of my childhood and innocence. My days were void of laughter and toys and wondering of what fun things would happen today, that was never a thought. Each day came with the sickening awakening thoughts of what the night had brought and wondering what the day would bring. My normal was whatever each day held and my days held fears, longing for a mom to love me to stay with me to talk with me to laugh with me and most of all protect me, but that was not to be. Instead, my mother sucked the very life and any love you may have thought about, right out of you.

School was awful for me as I was so shy and afraid to look anyone in the eye. I was very withdrawn which in today's society would have hailed with red flags; hell I would have been dressed in red from head to toe as I was a walking "red flag" of abuse and yet I was invisible in the eyes of others. Ever think about existing in a blind society? You look up as a child for acceptance a smile and no one sees you.

During first grade we had reading groups and if we did our reading out load and did it right we had a yellow chick placed by our name and this yellow chick was there throughout parent teacher conference. For those that did not read with the rest of the group and participate, they received a black bird to hang by their name. There by my name was a black bird and I was the only one with a blackbird. I stood out from the rest but not in a good way.

Today in school I fear that would be called child abuse as it down plays the importance of that child, it does not teach, it only demoralizes the person and re affirms their poor self image. They are the educators, how then should this child have been approached? I felt the astigmatism of the black bird all my life and every struggle I encountered there in my file box of memories stood the black bird to attest to my inabilities to do or be better or even OK for that matter. What movement the hand made in that instant to hang that black bird made a lasting negative impression on me.

On the farm I spent a lot of time in the barn helping with feeding chores and collecting eggs and cleaning the chicken house. There were days I stayed home from school to help plant potatoes and other garden produce. As for being around dad I did not have to worry about him touching me during the day, in fact it was so OK during the day I wondered what changed him when it got dark and wondered why it had to get dark. If the night had never come, then what dad and I had as a relationship would have been near perfect. He never yelled at me if I did, something wrong. He knew I was only trying to learn and be of help to him. I might have been young but I did understand that the only help dad had been Uncle Lewis and the chances of that were little to none. He would both be gone and stuck in the bar or having returned from the bar, would be too drunk to be of any help.

My brother could help but he had such a bad temper and no desire to be a part of the farming or anything so it became easier for my dad to take the easy way out and do it himself or solicit my help. I did not have the temper and I only wanted to be able to please anyone who asked anything of me, especially dad, as he did not yell.

Dad was the teacher of card games, the teacher of patience, the teacher of astrology and astronomy and wild flowers, and trees, knowing what the kinds of clouds were and what they meant. He had a master's degree in common sense and in fine humor and could beat anyone at a game of chess. He had the patients to teach others. Dad asked little of anyone. In addition; you could take him at face value, as I never knew him to lie.

Now I know you must be thinking I had dad on a shelf held higher than I should. Maybe at the time I did, and perhaps I had to do that to feel something was right. Maybe I had to learn to break down the bad and whoever did the least to me was the best, hell who knows. I do know that I have come full circle with a lot of my feelings. After years of soul searching and many tears I have learned to leave this in a gray area and let God decide where it belongs.

For a few years as a small child, I do remember in the evening during the summer dad, Lewis, and my brother would get out in the middle of the yard and throw the ball around. Playing bat the ball around was a part of their childhood memory. Athletics was a part of their life as they would often attend the country school for gymnastics in fact, Lewis taught gymnastics and he even help teach the ladies as well.

It was often said that Uncle Lewis was once the richest man in the county but that he had lost all of his money do to always drinking.

Neighbor Magie

Some days I would walk across the pasture, go over to the neighbors, and visit. If I could put up with the loud voice of Mark then I had a safe place to hang out and be away from mom. Maggie taught me how to sew and let me watch her make homemade rolls. She would clean the chickens for the fair, and scald a chicken to eat, and do each of these tasks all at the same time.

Her house was filthy and smelled of wet chicken feathers. There were flies everywhere, half-prepared food standing out on the cupboard amongst the flies and it was entirely possible to see, and smell half-scolded dead chickens in the kitchen sink. She could go from pulling feathers and guts to licking her fingers to rolling out dough and shaping it with her hands.

The apron Maggie wore was her towel to wipe dirty hands on, clean a dirty nose and to wipe a dish off. She was quick to insult my mom and hand me a fresh baked roll to eat covered in real butter. The rolls were good and something I never got at home, she fed me meals and it was nothing for her to pick at the leftovers on my plate or chew on my chicken bone if she seen a piece of meat that I did not get off the bone.

Often times I would help Maggie early in the morning pick cucumbers. We had to pick them by size, shape, and place into different baskets. We would haul the baskets up and down the rows as we picked and pitched the cucumbers into the baskets set out for each size. Sometimes I made as much as fifty cents in one day. It was nothing to fighting the mosquitoes out in the patch. The patch was in the middle of a field surrounded by trees.

I learned at an early age that Maggie did not wear underpants and one time she called and asked me to come over. When I got there, I had to help her do cucumbers again. We were bending over the cucumbers picking away, when she told me that she had sprayed mosquito spray between her legs she complained of burning and was dreading the ride to the cities to see her daughter as she was itching and burning so bad. She did not dare tell Mark, her husband and yet why was I privy to such information?

Mark always frightened me and perhaps he frightened her too I never gave that a thought. He was loud talking and rude. He was good to help with 4H and get kids involved but he had no personality to deal with kids. He did not even know how to talk to Maggie. One summer day when her and Mark were out in the field on the tractor and flat bed, she was driving the tractor and he was working with the bales when all of a sudden he started cussing her and yelling that she could drive better than that and she better listen and do it right. Maggie stopped the tractor, got off, and headed for the house. Mark was yelling every breath that matched her step cussing her to get back over there and drive tractor. She never looked back and I silently cheered from a peek hole within the grove.

While they were gone on vacation I was hired to fetch the mail in, feed the cats and dogs, feed the chickens, water the plants, and change the cattle between pastures twice a day by placing electric fence across the driveway so they could walk across the driveway. I did this for two weeks and was so proud that everything had gone well. When they returned, I received a ten-dollar bill. I was paid ten dollars and given a new shell to wear. I felt so special having made that kind of money and getting a new piece of clothing.

When I was about fifteen, my girl friend stayed over a night with me and I got to telling her about the nasty mess and smell in Maggie's house. She did not believe me so I drove her over there to prove to her how bad it was. She puked all the way down the driveway. The reason we ended up going over was Maggie needed me to squeeze into her laundry room as the door opened inward and she had packed it so full the door would barely open least wise not far enough for her to get through. Upon entering the kitchen, I yelled her name and she let me know she was in the bathroom cleaning and as I peeked around the door there bent over the tub exposing again Maggie's twat for the entire world to see. Of course, we had all we could do to keep from giggling.

Maggie did teach me how to sew she had patience with me and always praised and encouraged every stitch I took. I also knew that anyone she talked to she never failed to tell them that I was there and she was teaching me to sew, and if she took a notion, she would gossip about my mom as if I was not even in the room. I don't know if I ever felt the need to defend my mom but yet I did not like anything said about me as I felt I was only being laughed it. I always had a problem with thinking the worst but then that is all mom ever showed me was the worst and gave the least.

Maggie's world evolved around listening on the phone with a pair of binoculars and chewing fresh raw carrots. On a party line phone, it was so loud a deaf person could have heard it. There were no lines in her world that she would not cross. She would directly ask me if my mother was crazy, as she had heard from a reliable source that my mother was! How does a child of nine answer that, hell I thought mom was nuts a long time before that but it was not anything we would, could, or should talk about, as that would only be one more thing mom could add to the list of things that I had done wrong.

Rarely we would gather up the worms and maybe go fishing later that day. She sometimes would come down, sit at their pond, and watch over my brother and Paul, her son, and me. We knew the only way we would ever get to go swimming was if someone would be there to watch us and it usually was her or my dad. We were fine with either my dad or Maggie, as we could not stand the yelling and loud voice of Mark. There was no way we would have wanted mom around as she would have been passed out and would not have been able to save us anyway.

In midsummer we each had to choose a green pumpkin, carve our name into it, and watch it turn ripe with our name scabbed out on the pumpkin big and bold. We were always a part of this festive time and we had to taste the good pumpkin dessert made from the cooked pumpkins.

Violence was never very far from me in my life. In fact, life was a game of survival not a game of family outings and family prayers, or family meals. Nothing that I associate as being family was ever experienced when I was a child but then what did I know as we seldom had company and if we did they didn't come around for very long before they left.

What I thought was happening as a child, I learned after I grew up that it was not at all, as I had thought. Often times what we go through life thinking we are lost, may only be misplaced until a passage of time goes by and we can once again meet on a different playing field. Now I am not talking with the passage of a few hours or a few days but sometimes what we think is lost will return years later and be as a fine wine sipped as slow as the passage of time. You can learn that all is well and nothing was ever lost in fact sometimes love and respect was only stored away until it was safe to hand out to the rightful owner of it.

The Breakdown

I see my mom lying in bed, getting up when she felt like it, and doing what she wanted. She just existed in her world with what she wanted and if she did not want or like something she made it heard. I had to go to town with her to help her with laundry.

When I was around six years old mom suffered her first nervous breakdown and I was with her. We had gone to Tyler to the laundry mat as we never had owned a washer and a dryer If I carried the baskets in fast enough and ran out to get the detergent I could keep her from yelling. I got to fold clothes while she sat and smoked Pall Mall's and drank a soda. She was friendly to others that came in but always looked at me with disapproving eyes, eyes that I had grown to know so well. If I did not catch hell now, I would later. There was no comfort zone as a child, not a safe area that I as a child could enter into with my parents; I always had to figure her needs and moods out in order to find my own comfort. I learned early on in life that I would always come up short in her books, I grew to believe that there must be something wrong with me. I grew up feeling like a freak. She loved to tell me that I was the one lie that dad had told and I found myself on many occasions apologizing for having been born. Today I am ashamed of my weakness to have answered her in any way, shape or form. I wondered what did I have to do with any of their sexual encounters very little, I would say. No child asks to be born therefore a child is the last person that should be damned for ever having been born. So I will be damned if I will ever again say, "Mama don't be mad I am sorry that I was born." There damn you mother forever spewing your words on me, your hatred on me. Just damn you. No, I am not mad, because you do not know me you do not know how to take me but that is OK, perhaps by the end of this book you will have come to know who I am. No child ever asked to be abused. To be mad would only make me smaller than my enemies, to forgive is easy but now to forget is something I will never forget. To forget would be like driving at night without your headlights on and if you forget or do not have your headlights on then you are going to crash. I remember so I do not crash and I own my past as a map to my thoughts and a way of dealing with life today.

On this particular day as I was juggling the laundry basket and opening a car door, my mother dropped her basket of clothes and began to scream and held her head with both hands. She looked horrified! She looked around as if everything she knew or remembered was gone; she even wondered where she was. I ran through the alley to the back door of the medical clinic and got Dr Bob to come over to mom. Soon an ambulance came and hauled her off and Dr. Bob took me in his car up to the hospital. They did not allow me to go into her room. Nurses rushed in and out and whispered as they walked by. I looked to their eyes for reassurance, comfort, or whatever they had to offer but there were no smiles, and no kind words. I did not know if mom was dying or where I was supposed to go.

Soon my father came for me, still no hugs or smiles. I could not figure out what I had done wrong this time. Dad drove us out to the farm all the while telling me that I would have to go away for a while beings mom was sick. I cried and begged dad to let me stay home. I promised I would help cook and clean and most of all I did not want to be away from my dog. To no avail, I was sent to Iowa with Rod and Reba. By having to go down to Iowa and stay, I felt as though I was being punished for mom getting sick. I did not like being away from all that I knew.

Mom was rushed to Sioux City Iowa under the care of Dr. Kent. It was a mental hospital with locked wards and bars on the windows.

Coming Home and Seeing Mom

After a month or so, I was able to come home. I had remembered how I had to push a chair up to the stove, kneel on my knees, and cook food. Although I did not understand how the burners worked, I did remember how I had to be careful reaching over the burners to turn the knobs on. The first meal that I cooked was hamburgers and oatmeal for supper. Dave came up to the house just long enough to see what was for supper and informed me he was not eating burned pig slop.

Every Saturday morning I was to wash and wax the living room, dining room, and kitchen floors on my hands and knees. Although I do not remember when I first got that job from mom I knew that I had to do that no matter what. With her gone I did not have her sitting there snapping her gum, smoking, and watching for me to make a mistake so she could point it out. Looking back, I think she would have actually been mad if I had not made a mistake or missed a spot. After I dusted the furniture, she would walk along the buffet edge, check for dust, and look at the bottom rung of the buffet to see if I had missed a spot. Not once was anything about the good I did but only the bad I did. Seeing good was not in her realm of selections.

When I got my chores done I could play with my dog, Blackie, and the litter of pups. I had to keep them in the porch. I had to clean up the dirty papers off the porch floor and lay fresh down after the pups made a mess. I did not like that much but I did not complain, as I wanted the pups nearby. They were always glad to see me and they loved me, no matter what they loved me. I did think about mom and wonder where she was at and if she missed me. Maybe I hoped that she would miss me and be glad to see me. It had seemed so long ago that we had seen mom.

Playing with the dogs took my mind off mom and her condition that I still did not understand. The dogs made no demands and loved unconditionally. There was no fear that she was going to jerk the door open and start yelling at me. I lived in fear of her every command as there was no laughter when it was her and I. Perhaps I was a reflection of her as a lost child and she had to see how much I could take or if she could break me. I really do not know why she had me, well yes I do it was all a big mistake and a lie according to her. A heart filled with contempt cannot possibly find room to love.

On Sunday my dad announced that he was driving us to Sioux City to see mom. At last minute my brother did not go so it was just dad and I. It took so long to get there and I could not wait to see my mom. I colored and hummed to myself to kill time hanging out in the middle of nowhere and concentrating on nothing. Finally, we arrived for our visit.

We walked up the big steps and down the hall. Mom was sitting in a waiting room. The room was lined with chairs, the big green ones with shinny arms, the chairs had no back legs on them and I remember they were like the chairs in the Tyler Clinic. The chairs swayed towards the floor with the weight of mom in it. I ran up to her saying, "Hi mom!" She abruptly pushed me away and I seen that same fear in her eyes. She yelled, "Who are you, I don't know you!" My dad sat down nearby and said, "This is our daughter Marynell." Mom had no clue who I was. Dad kept gently talking to her about what he had been doing. Soon a nurse came and took me out into the hallway. No smiles only piercing eyes, again I wondered what I had done. No one explained anything to me. I sat out in a bare waiting room and scared to death. I wondered how long it would be before dad come to me. Was I going to be all alone again? Was dad going to stay in there? There were no answers to anything as a child but there were a lot of questions.

The drive home was quiet and uneventful. Things around home stayed pretty much the same. I did the best I could which I realize now was not good. Home for the most part consisted of Dad and I. There were no counselors or helping hands of guidance on how we should deal with this unknown territory, we were now beginning to tread on.

On rainy days or snowy blizzard days, dad and I would often play cards. He taught me how to play crazy 8, muggings, whist, and cribbage and oh yes a card game called ninety-nine. The first time I lost very badly at cards I got mad, threw the cards on the floor, and cried. The next day when I asked him to play he would not. It was quite a few days before we played again. He shuffled the cards and informed me that if I threw a tantrum like I had last time, he would not play cards with me again. He explained that I had to learn to lose, that I was not always going to win, and that no one wanted to play with a sore loser. With warning in hand we commenced to playing cards, one game after another and I had learned the lesson at hand on how not to be a sore loser. This lesson would help me not just at cards but also at life in general. In all the difficulties in life, I never felt like a loser but I did feel lost.

Mom Comes Home

Soon mom was able to come home and when she did, it was not the same. When she came through the door, she looked around so lost and scared. "Did we get new furniture? I do not remember any of this." I giggled as our couch and chairs were old, we had never had new furniture. The overstuffed rocker that she often had sat in with one leg threw over the arm, looked sagged and lopsided from her hours of sitting in that chair smoking, why there was even burn marks where she had fallen asleep or sat in a stupor dropping her cigarette only to burn a hole in the chair. The pattern on the arm was worn smooth from the weight of her leg.

Dave and I started bouncing a basketball in the kitchen when from out of nowhere she started yelling, "Stop it, stop it, please stop it." She was holding her head. We could not figure out what her problem was we were doing what we use to do. Dad hurried over and took the ball away from us and informed us that things had changed; we were to no longer bounce balls in the house or make any noise as it bothered mom. We just did not understand why she had changed. We didn't understand until years later when we learned that during her stay in the hospital she had received fifty two electric shock treatments, shock treatments that not only knocked out her reasons for being depressed but her complete memory of her life, dad, and us kids. It was a long slow journey for her to get her memory back and the first thing that returned was the things that depressed her, not her happy memories or maybe there just had never been any

happy memories to remember. No, there was no
not of her family or her life on the farm. To look i.
there were no signs of happiness, love, or acceptance

I am sure it was scary for her to learn bits and p.
her past, her fears, and remembering various things
life. To me it seemed like mom was putting a puzzle tog
only the pieces never came out right and yes, there
pieces missing. Like the love of a mom, the pride of a mc
the teachings of a mom, loving her family, cooking for h
family. Now life changed, she got up whenever she wanted
she left when she wanted, she came home when she wanted
and most of all she did what she wanted. She was a non-
participant in our lives. She was not accountable to anyone
or for anything. We had to figure out how to fit into her life.

There were no tickle games, no cuddling games, and no
fishing trips with mom along. One time we talked her into
going and she passed out in the back seat of the car from all
her tranquilizers and sleeping pills. She did not even
remember going. We could have just as well left her home.
We did not go to church as a family; we did not go out to eat
as a family. We did not sit down and eat our meals at home
as a family. There was nothing that I can remember ever
doing as a family. We did not say grace at the table. We did
not fit the modern day definition of a family in modern day
society of the late 50's or early 60's or 70's or 80's. .

As mom began to find her way around again and learn
who she was since having lost her memory, she began to run
around and staying away from home. When she left the
mental hospital, they gave her prescriptions for tranquilizers,
diet pills, and sleeping pills. Before long, she was taking
thirty-six pills a day. Mom had to go and see counselors
about her depression and she would come home and say
things like, "Shit they are crazier than me those damn fools."
She did not get anything out of going to sessions. It is so true
when they say smart like a fox. She fooled the world over
and she was good at her game. The game was the only thing
she was good at perhaps because we were all of her private
game pieces and she played us, used us, and tossed us,

hatever fit the game. No price was too high for her to pay. I now this because I counted the pills and sometimes I would ide them but always put them back as I was scared of her. It was not until years later that I learned she was diagnosed as a manic-depressive. She had endured the fifty-two electric shock treatments and she would have to have them from time to time. I did not understand how she could feel depressed, as she did not have a worry in the world. Dad catered to her when she was home and even served her coffee in bed every morning that she was there. She never had to shovel snow; she never had to leave in a cold car as he always had it warmed up for her. From my shoes life had to be good for her and yet I could see the misery and depression.

I'm Cold Daddy

It was unusually cold that evening and the 12-inch-by-12-inch metal grate above the oil furnace was no match for the North West winds that sailed through the upstairs windows like a fan blowing. Thank goodness I was able to close Dave's room as he usually slept out in the trailer with Lewis.

I had a mattress with a hole in it that I had stuffed clothes in to try to keep the broken spring from scratching my legs. The blankets were torn and leaking batting, I would fold them repeatedly, usually curl up, and chill my way to feeling warm. On this particular night, I could not get warm, and I could not sleep. The wind was howling through the trees and it sounded awful, maybe there was someone out there. Finally, I had myself so cold and so scared I ran down stairs and crawled into bed with dad. He was nice and warm and I snuggled up to his hump back to get warm. Soon he turned over, faced me, and hugged me close. As this happened his breathing changed, it was heavier. He began to rub between my legs and rock back and forth into me. I felt all sorts of funny feelings, I just wanted to get warm and go to sleep, but that is not what happened. He pulled my panties to the side of my leg and crushed me with his body and it hurt me, soon I felt warmth run all over me between my legs. He told me to put my pajamas on and go to sleep. I was hurting and I had to go use the bathroom. It was there I found blood coming from me. I was so scared and I did not understand. I returned to bed with him but soon the kitchen door opening awakened me.

Uncle Lewis yelled for dad. He was telling him to get out there. I woke dad up and told him Lewis was in the kitchen yelling for him. As dad entered, the kitchen a very drunk Lewis stood there wobbling and hanging onto the kitchen chair, he started yelling at dad, "Do you know where your wife is? I know damn well she is running around with other men and I want to know what you are going to do about it?" "It is none of your damn business what my wife is doing. Now I want you out of here. I have put up with you and your drunk ass long enough. I don't care where you go but you cannot stay here any longer."

Lewis suddenly moved across the kitchen and grabbed dad around the throat pushing him into the cupboard. I grabbed a big butcher knife from the container of knives that hung on the wall; I pushed it into his back, "You leave my dad alone. You let go of him." They immediately stopped and turned to stare at me and to take the knife away, I was crying and shaking as I thought Lewis was going to kill my dad.

Dad made coffee, we sat at the kitchen table, and you cannot talk to a drunk so we listened to a drunk instead. All of this was the straw that broke the camel's back; Dad was through putting up with him. Just then my mom came home. "Hi what is going on, is there something wrong?" With that dad told her they would talk later. While she had been out pleasing other men, I, the child, was pleasing my father and my reward. At least that is how it has been stuck in my head, was her smelling like booze and handing me a pair of red glass shoes. "This is for being so good." This will always be frozen in my mind. Was I given the shoes because I had performed her job for her so she would not have to service dad, or was it a payment in kind out of guilt? I got the shoes for having put up with what dad did. Between mom's red lipstick and now these red shoes, I hated the color red. Red to me is the color of her, a whore. When the red lipstick came out it only meant that she was leaving and Lord only knows when she would return. I would ask her to stay home or if she wanted to play a game but of course, she was way too busy. She was too busy to be giving any of her precious time to me. When I asked her for help with my school work she had no time for that either. I do not have one memory of her helping me with homework.

Life Goes On

Mom continued with a life style of tranquilizers, running to the bars and laying off the house chores onto me. I hated being around her because she was so mean and I hated it when she left because I had no one to protect me. I had no one and yet everyone had me.

Sometimes, I would clean Lewis's trailer for 50 cents. It was away for me to earn money. Most times, he would leave me alone but sometimes, he would try to dig in my panties or lay me back on the bed and rub hard on me and press into me hurting my pelvic bone. All I wanted was to earn some money, I did not like being pressed against a cupboard or trying to dig in my panties. Most of all I hated not being able to tell anyone, or was this normal, is this what other kids went through? Why were the other kids smiling and I was not? I did not like what I was going through. Sometimes, it was a matter of fighting off Lewis by day and dad by night. Now it was to the point my dad would come upstairs, I would stay curled in a tight ball, and he would breathe funny and rub on me. Sometimes I would hide under the bed or in the closet and try to stay awake and listen for him to come up the steps. He would stand by the side of the bed, ejaculate, moan, and groan. I would hide behind the vacuum cleaner. Why was this happening, why wasn't Dave sleeping in the house, in his room, at least if he was here dad would not come upstairs. There was no one for me to turn to and no one I could talk to. I didn't want to talk to anyone as I was to ashamed, I only wanted it all to stop.

I never went back down to his bed again but dad did continue to come back upstairs and try to make me a part of his sexual urges. To this day I need not even close my eyes and all is present when I allow myself to think about it. All the smells, the noises, the scary moaning and groaning that I had to hear, smell, and receive against my will. What was I to do whom I tell? Who then will protect me? Certainly not a question I asked myself. To this day, I still have a hard time describing what he did to me. I guess because it is so ugly to say. Maybe all the ugliness that spilled all over me is what made me feel like such a freak and so ugly when I was growing up. Why didn't mom just stay home where she belonged, why didn't dad make her stay home? Why did Lewis totally ignore me not even speak to me only when he wanted to rub all over me or grab at me he would go out of his way to hunt me down and look for a chance to touch me? Now I did ask these questions. I had anger and a fear of my mother like no other feeling I had experienced. I was angry because she never stayed home, I was angry because she never had the time of day for me; she never smiled at me, never hugged me or gave me personal encouragement. As for the men in my life, not one I could confide in not one man took up for me but more than one man took me took all of me sometimes both in the same day. Was I not worth loving and being good to?

The Priest and the First of Many

I remember the first man mom brought out to the house. Father Bert. On that first time he was out, which mom had driven him out; he drank wine and got drunk. Mom was gone forever taking him home and my dad never said anything. I guess she figured I would not know what was going on. Funny no adult ever thinks about the fact that when you literally throw a child into an adult world, that child is no longer innocent with innocent thoughts, you are aware of breathing patterns, smells, and looks. It is a feeling like no other that you get in your gut and it never leaves you. You cannot put your finger on it and there is no one word that describes that feeling but when you get that feeling in your stomach you had better listen to it. It is your only defense against wrong, it is telling you that things are not as they appear to be, you are not safe with this person or where you are at. To this day, my stomach is my best indicator.

I have no way of knowing if dad knew what was going on or not but I am sure it would have been easy to assume that nothing was going on with a priest. After all, shouldn't a man of the cloth be above reproach?

On another occasion a man came out to the farm shortly after mom had arrived home, he was laying on the horn, which woke me, and he was drunk. By then I was down stairs and I heard my dad tell him that she was his wife and that he had to leave, not yelling just stating in fact! In the end, dad and I had to help push and shovel the guy out as he had been stuck in the yard. Not a word was said. Dad was not mad and mom did not seem any meaner, in fact, she even went out again, where I do not know. Why didn't dad make her leave or yell at her or do something? I think now as I look back that dad probably figured he could get no one else so he would put up with what is.

Then there was Ray, and another from the ASC office in Marshall and another from Ruthton and from Pipestone. One of her "male friends" worked at a local radio station and mom would hang on every song and wait for his mentioning her in their private code. Like a teenager, she would swoon to the radio. Another friend was from Florence, and then there was Jim from Marshall. There were so many I lost count and forgot half the names.

Between the family reunions and being forced to go upstairs with cousin Weston at his home and being molested by him, and being molested by dad, uncle Lewis and verbally abused by mom. Nothing was done as a whole but a lot was done by fragmented pieces. There were pieces of me strewn everywhere and near everyone. So many had taken bits and pieces of me and kept for their own pleasures and vice.

Out Cold

I knew mom had all kinds of pills and would take them anytime she felt like it but I did not know just how it affected her until one night I was sitting in the dining room watching T. V. and mom was sitting on the couch in the living room. I heard this sick moan almost like a cow when it is in labor. I looked back and mom had drool running from her mouth and she was slowly falling forward. She fell, hit the coffee table in front of her, and down onto the floor. She did not move, just laid there. I screamed and threw my pop bottle I had; I thought she had died. Dad came in from the kitchen and said for me to help him. We dragged her off to bed and I mean drag, as she was every bit of 230 lbs and dead weight. We both struggled to throw her head and arms on the bed and then lift and push her body the rest of the way. Finally, we got her covered up.

For the first time that I remember and at the age of nine, I stood up to dad and asked him why he let her take that stuff. I was mad at him for letting her. He explained that it was either that way or she would not sleep all night; and which would I rather have. Like I had any say. I knew that was the end of the conversation. I hated it and I will never forget it she felt so clammy and cold. I could not stand to touch her. I just realized how long it had been since I had touched her.

Of course, I always had to wash her back and scrub it good but I always made sure that the rag was between her and my skin. I did not like to look at her naked body, as there were several scars, and sagging skin. For many years there were many men, drugs, moods, and the abuse she put me through. She felt so cold and lifeless her eyes were so filled with that far away look, I often wondered where she was in her head. She looked void of content and full of emptiness.

.

Jim

One of many of her friends! He and dad would talk and have coffee together and then he would take my mom to where ever they were going and he would come back and sleep on our couch. Sometimes he would come out and stay every weekend or every other weekend. I was given orders to be nice to him as he was a nice man, I became more rebellious as I resented the fact that she could laugh and talk nice to him and even talk nice to me like I mattered when I never did before. It was so easy for me to be a snob and rude maybe because of my age and maybe because it was the only way I could push her buttons. On a couple occasions, Jim threatened to leave because I did not make him feel wanted. He would eventually settle down and always try to give me some money to spend. I personally did not give two shits and a damn for him or his money. I only found it easy to resent what he had and I did not like to see her show Jim the love and the smiles from my mom, love and smiles that she never gave us kids. In time, she grew tired of him and I noticed that her mood towards him was rude and cold. When I look back, I think it was because he tried to control her, where she went and if she went out and expected her to answer to him. Sometimes I would over hear them having an argument but pretending to be fine, the minute dad came through the door. Jim was a fake, rich asshole who thought his money and smelly cigars and fancy car could wine and dine anyone he wanted to.

When I did go along with him and mom he would try to buy me things, I knew he was trying to buy my friendship, I was not for sale never have been and still am not to this day. All I have is me and at the end of life, there shall be no one that can ever say that I sold out for a price. He would buy meat from my dad for his daughter and give dad cash. I always looked at it as he was paying for what he got off my mom. He would take her to Watertown S. D. and stay a weekend on the pretense of bringing home a bottle lamb for me. I did receive the bottle lamb but I learned years later that they would stay in a motel room together and not with her drinking friends brother that had the sheep. How they could come home and face my dad I will never know. Jim even bought her clothes as if she was his wife, what must dad have thought?

On one occasion, I ended up in the hospital because of her and her temper. She had come home from town only to find I had not washed two cups and a dish. I remember just freezing in my spot above the chicken house where I had been playing. She stood on the edge of the step with the broom in her hand and screaming at me to get my ass in the house now. I peeked out the window frame and I felt like she could see right through me. I instantly backed up and started running to the other end of the chicken house lengthwise with the boards and all of a sudden I fell between the boards and my leg was stuck above my knee. Ouch! It hurt so badly and I could not get free. There was no sense in yelling for help as she would never come up here anyway and if she did, she would beat the shit out of me while I was stuck there.

The only feeling I had other than pain was the warmth of my tears silently rolling down my cheek. Trying to cry quietly so mom would not hear me. Mom ended up leaving for town and no there was no one around to help free me as dad was working out in the field and Lewis was at the bar in town.

Finally, I was lose and made it up to the house. Dad returned from the field and started feeding chores; Lewis returned and was up in the barn too. I was in the house and limping around. I noticed my leg was swollen tight inside my jeans and I could no longer stand on my leg. Eventually I crawled up to the barn screaming, crying as it hurt so bad, and I was scared. Dad came out and Lewis followed, they could see it was bad and dad took Lewis's car and took me to the emergency room in Tyler. After several x-rays, they cut my pants off me and told dad that I would have to have surgery in the morning that the inside of my knee was full of blood clots. I was so scared I did not know what to expect.

I went into surgery by myself. When I awoke, I could see a drain tube running from my knee to over the side of the bed and into a container on the floor. The rest of my knee was bandaged looking huge. It hurt so badly I lay there crying and wondering where mom was. Finally, a nurse came in, looked everything all over, and rubbed my face with her nice smelling hand. She brought me some medicine for pain and told me to try to sleep.

Later that same day mom and Jim came to visit and to tell me they were going to Watertown and would bring me back a bottle lamb. When I awoke later that evening there was an ugly man standing in my door way and grinning at me. The nurse pulled him away and he went into the next room where I learned later his wife was. Every day at visiting time, he would stop by my room and I was so scared he was going to hurt me.

Nine days come and went and no visitors. Dad finally came and took me home. I thought I was never going to get home again. To this day, I have a permanent dent on the inside of my knee and I can feel where there is a wedge of bone missing.

As soon as I got home the chore list started, nothing had changed. The only change was I had more animals to love. I loved my lambs and feeding them. Dad gave me the milk to feed them and the knowledge of what to look for. I was so proud of how big they were getting and how well I was taking care of my lambs. Dad would do the morning feeding until I was up but as the years went by I soon took over on all the feedings and the money I earned was how I bought my school clothes.

Cousin Weston

I was probably five when that started and it did not stop until I was 14 years old. It started when our family reunions were held at his parent's home. His mother would always tell us to go upstairs and watch Mickey Mouse cartoons until it was time to eat. We were to stay out of the way and be good kids! Good kids, I guess, meant to being abused and keeping our mouth shut. Although it was not a daily or even a weekly thing, it was there any time he might be around and he would see to it that I was alone with him eventually. The last time was when I was babysitting for a lady he was dating. It is odd to say that he was dating as he really involved himself with ladies that had small children. The small children were all he was really interested in getting close to.

He would pick me up and take me to town to baby sit, which appeared on the surface to make sense as he only lived a couple miles from where I lived and it was on his way. The return trip home became ugly and abusive. He would not take me straight home but rather take me to the Arco Park. It was there that the sexual abuse became more violent, repulsive, and lasting longer. He would place my hands in his pants, hold my hand on his, and make me pull back and forth and hold my head down and against him. He would push my face down as he ejaculated and let his filth run all over my hands and rub some on my face. It was in the dark of the night, in that silence that I silently screamed inside with fear and not knowing where I could run to or who I could talk to. It was in that park that when the evil deed was done that he would lead me to the water's edge and clean his slime off me. Having been sexually abused in the dark while Mickey Mouse movies played, and going to the Arco Park where I was molested on several occasion, are bad memories to this day.

I only see sexual abuse and the memories of such when I see or hear Mickey Mouse. A character like that should be a loving memory and a source of fairy wonderland for a child but it is only one of my worst nightmares. Weston would tell me that I wasn't very pretty but that I could be his girl and he would be good to me. I hated him and I to this day hate any reminder of Mickey Mouse.

My life was filled with nightmares and no fairy tales or wonderland. Who could I possibly tell about this sexual abuse when I suffered sexual abuse at my very own home and in my father's bed as well as my own bed? Mom would not believe me but would probably blame me and for sure, she would rejoice in the joy of telling my dad and having something to say about his family, as she never missed a chance to run them down. She would not be the least bit concerned about me. Everything that happened or went wrong in life was her ticket to see what she could get out of the situation and by that, I mean sympathy. She never ever could see or feel things from the victim's point but rather it was all about what was in it for her.

I knew that Weston was molesting the three children that I was babysitting and I didn't know how to protect them. I did protect them when I was there; I never let him get them alone. When he would coax them into the bedroom to play a game of tickle I would go in too and throw myself down between him and the kids as I did not want him touching them. I didn't want him touching me either but I would rather it be me then to have to watch him touch them.

Weston kept abusing children from all areas. He abused even his own children. The day before aunt April died she had told me that Ann, Weston's mom had told her how wonderful Weston was and how April's son had abandoned his children. She cried to me that she thought Weston was bothering her granddaughters. I informed her that he was. It was the next morning I learned she had died of a heart attack, more like a broken heart.

The day of her viewing Weston was there and tried to take my daughter out of my arms. I held her so close to me I feared I might have crushed her legs but I knew one thing for sure; he was not going to touch my daughter. As I viewed the casket and seeing the top half of April's face, I starred at it and silently and made a promise to her that he would not get away with what he was doing, not anymore. His mother, Ann, my aunt, would soon find out what a precious piece of shit her son was.

A couple days after the funeral I called child protection services in Marshall and told them I had this abuse to report. In doing this, I had to relive again the sexual abuse that Weston had put me through years ago. They said if the girls did not admit to the abuse I would then have to testify to what I had gone through years ago. While I was scared, I was more hurt at having seen April cry so hard her last day on earth, I only said, "Go for it."

The county attorney was also the city attorney where Weston worked. Now right there was a conflict of interest but of course, I did not know that at the time. Cecil, the county attorney, really did not want Weston to go to jail or for this to become public because he needed Weston in a rural water lawsuit the city had going on. In fact, Weston was the key witness for the city. I am sure Cecil wished like hell this could have been swept under the rug. He did not know the size of my broom! I talked with him on different occasions and told him I wanted him put away to never hurt another child. Cecil informed me that this was only a first offense and that there would be no jail time but maybe some probation and taking courses on how not to do this again. I tried in vain to tell him how your childhood is robbed. You no longer see innocence, you may not be able to verbalize it but you look at people close to you and you worry they will touch you. You have been thrown into an adult world of hands and penis and heavy breathing. That does not compute with playing freely as a child.

After the trial, Cecil called me all happy with his success and that Weston got probation, assigned a probation officer, and had to comply with the judge's orders. All of this meant nothing to me only strengthened my resolve. I immediately called the Marshall newspaper and affirmed that what happened in court was now of public record. I requested that they publish the record of Weston's court findings in the newspaper. This was my way of protecting other children and warning their parents of what Weston had done and would do if given the chance. I also wanted to make sure his mother read about her precious son. I wanted her to hurt but I knew she would never hurt like what I hurt but it was a start. I also hoped that it ate at her conscious if she had one as to what she had last said to April. I am sure to this day; she never knew that I knew her last words to her sister.

A few people know I was the one that reported him but the granddaughters, my cousins, do not know. I had hoped to be able to tell them one day of my last conversation with their grandmother and how she knew and worried herself to death literally over the girls. The girl's mom aligned herself beside Weston, she sold out for the attention he would give her; she never figured out that he only hung around her to get to the children.

Within two weeks of his verdict, I made it a point to drive past the Arco Park and sure enough there he was and he had the girls all to himself with his little camper. Nothing had changed! I immediately remembered that a second offense would send him to jail. That following Monday I went to the Marshall courthouse and waited to talk to the probation officer. I told him who I was and what role I had played in the case brought against Weston. I also told him that if he wanted to get the second charge I could take him right out to the park and show him right where they were. He then informed me I had to let it go and not worry about it. I informed him he needed to do his G damn job. I was shaking I was so mad.

There was no support from my husband, the cop; he really did not want me to bring the case. Hell couldn't have stopped me as I lost so much and not to mention my beautiful aunt that I had grown so close to. Maybe I couldn't protect or help myself as a child but I sure could help someone else even if it was from behind the scenes. To me if you have knowledge that something wrong is going on and you say nothing then to me you are as guilty as the person doing wrong. Now I do not view others in that same light but I view me in that light. In my heart of hearts if I can help someone then I must do so or I am no better than the one doing wrong.

I did learn later that Sam and his wife were proud of me and that meant the world. Pride was not a familiar word in my life. Sam and his wife had been friends for a few years and he was a part time cop that knew what was going on but his hands were tied as he could not get any help out of the local sheriff's office. Sam was there to help clean up the mess of what Weston had left. Their pride in me for what I had taken on was the first pride I had ever felt from anyone and it felt good. Funny how far a few kind words can go and how much drive it can give you to keep going no matter how hard the task may be.

Death

A few years had passed and we had moved away from the area. One day the phone rang and it was Sam. He wanted to offer me his sympathy and right away, I wondered what he meant. He said, "You haven't heard? "I said, "No, heard what?" "Well Weston is dead." "Good" I said. Sam continued, "He was caught again and today the sheriff came to deliver papers on him and he knew this meant jail this time. While the sheriff was at the front door with the warrant, Weston went out through the garage and grabbed the chain saw. He then drove the city truck down to the little building under the bridge and locked himself in the city shed. He started the saw, placed it in the vice, leaned into, and cut his throat nearly all the way through. "Wonderful now he will not ever hurt anyone again." Sam's wife was not happy like I was, as she wanted to see him go to jail and suffer at the hands of prisoners. After all we all know how prisoners feel about child molesters. Even hardened criminals have their own ethics when it comes to harming a child.

I had started a snowball that exposed years of abuse by one man, I can name at least 30 of his victims, and I am willing to bet there are nearly a hundred more that I have no knowledge about. Do I feel bad? No, not at all. Would I do it again? Without a doubt, I would do it again and I would make sure there is no hidden agenda by a county attorney. I personally feel that the county attorney and the probation officer should have been held accountable as they had the knowledge and the means to put an end to this. If an end would have been put to Weston's action then the victims from that point on would not have had to suffer. How they sleep at night is beyond me. They too will face their judgment day and God does not forget. A license to practice in judgment should never mean it is a license to turn their back on something because of a hidden agenda. It does not mean being able to turn your back on your morals if you have any. If there are no morals then I only feel sorry for their empty soul.

Religion through the Years

I had to go to Sunday school and attend church but I did not like it, as I felt so alone. The only thing I did like about Sunday school was the teachers not the kids. My aunt April was one of the teachers and she always said hi and smiled at me. Then there was Pearl and Joy that always made me feel loved and OK.

More times than I care to remember I would walk the nearly two miles to attend Sunday school and church as mom was either in bed yet or gone. Dad was not usually finished up with milking chores and could not quit just to take me. Sometimes I got a ride from a couple while I was walking up to church. They were very kind people and never made me feel like I was a burden. I felt like an orphan which I could have just as well have been as there were very few times that anyone went with me to church.

The few times my mom did attend church she was usually high on pills or had the hang over affect from the sleeping pills, either way she was not something to feel proud of. Sometimes she would get the giggles in church and I would be telling her to hush. I really do not know what was worse sitting in a pew all alone or near Mrs. Tom as she worried I might touch her coat. She would glare at me and then pull her coat away and brush at it. I know I never had touched it and I know too that that was her worst fear. When I would leave the country church walking I would go down by the hall and take the gravel road out to the county road that I walked home. On this particular day as I got near the parsonage I seen a gray kitten with white paws. He soon bounced out at me and tried to follow me down the road. No matter what I did, the cat trailed along. I carried the kitten home and decided to name the kitten Reverend beings it had been up at the church. I loved animals and hated to see anything left out in the cold and all alone, I guess it is because that is the way I felt, left out in the cold and all alone.

I continued with my religious studies all the while feeling like it was for everyone else and not for me. For me it was as if I was standing on the outside of the church looking in and seeing everyone else connected, connected to each other, to church, and to friends. I saw myself as being disconnected from them and from myself and my so called family. Many times, I stood outside the church trying to make my way through the crowd that stood right in front of the door to chat. I would look up trying to catch an eye or a smile but a child is often over looked in a crowd of adults.

When confirmation classes started, they were on a Wednesday night out at Diamond Lake church and sometimes at the Arco Lutheran church. This is just one more group that I did not feel a part of. I did not have their loving mother, I did not have their nice clothes, I was not a welcome part of their friendship and laughter. I hated being here and not feeling included. I felt like I was tolerated at best. Sometimes when mom would pick me up from class, she would take me from there to the Florence Bar with her and I would have to sit and watch her shake dice, snap her fingers to the music, suck on Pall Mall's and flirt with whoever would give her the time of day. She would let me have a pop and some peanuts, even play the jute box it was basic bribery to keep me happy, not complain, and not tell dad. Her personality would soon change when it was time to go home. She would become mean and sad again. I would ride quietly next to her. She hated the farm, she hated to be a wife, she hated to be a mother, she only loved the attention of others period the end, that was the way it was. Mom could not have loved herself. To her love was all about being "out there."

59

I truly did not know where I fit in the scheme of things. I guess I could have tried to talk to kids but my conversation would have been about abuse, alcoholism, a crazy mother that took me to the bar. I don't think they could have comprehended what my life was like. I had a mom that regretted ever having me and regretted having to spend time with me. I was her living pain in the ass and she reminded me daily. I was the girl that should have been named Trojan.

Trojan

From the time, I can remember mom would tell me that I was the one lie my dad told. She would say things like, "You think your dad is so great and perfect, you are the one lie he told." Then when I got older, she would tell me that my name should have been Trojan as that was the lie my dad told. He had told her he had a rubber on and he did not and because of that, I was born. I think that is where her hate for me lay; I was to have never been. She had a rough time bringing Dave into the world, because of this there were to be no more children. Low and behold, along I came and she and I both had a rough time. She resented me, as I was the cause of her rough time when mom was in one of her more evil moods she would often say, "You love dad more than me and I bet you would pick him over me if we were to divorcee." Why wouldn't I? What was there to choose from? I remember telling her I was sorry and please do not be mad at me. I also learned that I was to be quiet, not get in the way. I was always in the way, I learned later I was only in her way and no one else but I did not learn that until I was in my late 40's. It was one of many scars left on me.

Mom used to tie me in a rocking chair with a dishtowel, I would rock my way through the living room, dining room and on into the kitchen. She would turn me around again, and I would rock my way back. Probably why I am somewhat hump back as I was also told there was no back support to sit me up straight. The whole purpose in doing this was to keep me from being anymore work to her then necessary. The less she had to do with me the better. Even as

I got older and maybe someone stopped by like the Avon lady, if I tried to be in the same room with them mom would look at me and say, "If we say something I think you should hear I will put it in a jar and save it for you." She always would embarrass me. I know now that she only succeeded in making herself look bad. I still felt like I had to apologize for her behavior or for her saying something cruel to someone else. I know it was not my place but I guess it goes along with me always feeling guilty for every thing and for every outcome.

Mabel

Mabel and her husband Clark used to come out to our house and visit along with their children. Clark was stationed in the military with my dad and had been with dad when dad met mom. Clark and dad were best friends and wrote to each others families while in the military. Mabel told me years later that they quit coming out because she (Mabel) could not stand to see the way I was treated, that and my mother would flirt with Clark. Mabel did not care for my mom at all. Who could blame her? Mom's whole world was about attention and it had to be attention spent on her.

Mabel and I became very close during 1981 through 1985 during which time I was going to college in Marshall where she lived. I would often run down to her home during my long breaks between classes. We would share stories, love and laughter. I loved her hugs because they were tight and real. I always felt loved there. In fact, my daughter's middle name is Mabel and that is after my dear friend. I have so much respect for Mabel as she did not have a rich easy life. After her husband died of cancer, Mabel was all alone to raise her children. She did this by having her beauty shop right in her home so she was always available for her children. In my eyes, she is such a respectable person, loving mother, and an accomplished businesswoman. I feel blessed so blessed to have gotten back with her and having learned about her as a person, a mother and my dear friend. To this day I have nothing but the utmost respect for her.

Glad to Be Leaving Home

I can still see mom and how she stood in front of the mirror that hung outside the bathroom in the kitchen. I watch her from behind as she painted her lips bright red and putting her makeup on and telling me to feed dad his supper and to get to bed on time. When I asked her if she could help me with my homework she said no she had to go and that I should get dad to help me. She never once helped me with schoolwork, she never even looked at my schoolwork, and she never once put me to bed, or even come upstairs to tuck me in. She seldom was home when I went to bed. Now when I think back, she threw me at dad. She had no time for family but had all her time to give to total strangers that she would sooner or later turn into her one night stands or for longer if they gave her the attention that she wanted. It is sad when you think about how empty she was and shallow she was.

Silently I screamed on the inside at her, as I hated her for leaving me. I was scared of the nighttime. Today I do not hate her as I have learned and believe down to my core that bitterness and hatred are more harmful to yourself than what anyone can do to you. I have also learned that no one can take anything from you unless you give it to them and I did not give anything to them, they did take from me but I never gave it to them.

In the darkness I strained my eyes starring towards the doorway in hopes that dad would not walk through. However, he did whenever he felt like it and he would kneel by the bed and ask me in a low voice if I was sleeping. He would moan and breathe funny and touch me all over and sometimes crawl into bed with me. Even if I just lay tightly pulled together he would rub all over me and pry my legs apart. When he would leave I had the job of wiping his enjoyment off of me then I would hide in the back of my closet behind the old vacuum cleaner that stood upright and tall. I would curl up tight, cry, and look towards the open closet entrance.

Morning would come and he would yell upstairs for me to get up it was time to go to school. He would talk to me and we would play cards after school. I would go out into the barn and help him. It was almost as if nothing ever happened at night except I knew that it had.

Mom never woke me for school; she never got out of bed. She would start yelling for me to get down to the bus as much as ½ hour earlier than the bus was to come. She did not want me in the house at all. Many times, I stood at the end of the driveway freezing cold just to be out of her way and away from her yelling voice. When I returned from school, she would be gone and I hated that, as I did not know what might happen to me. If it was not for the bad nights all alone in the dark, dad and I could manage the farm and chores. After all, I was the one in the barn, in the hog house, in the chicken house, in the field loading and unloading corn fodder and hauling bales of straw in. Dad and I would bring loads of bales in and load them on the conveyer. He would get into the haymow and I would line the bales up on the conveyer to roll up into the loft.

I did love the farm, being outside, and especially working with dad. He was so appreciative even the time we were out in the middle of the cow yard and he decided that I could learn how to pull the pulley ropes up so he could get the hay in the haymow. He quickly showed me the clutch, the gears and the direction that he wanted me to drive and that he would yell for me to stop. I was sure that I could handle this job. I had to wait for dad to get up in the barn and finally I saw him motioning for me to pull the tractor slowly forward. This was not going well as the cows were closing in around the tractor and standing in front of the tractor, I worried that I might hit the cows. They just would not move. All of a sudden dad was up on the tractor beside me saying, "damn it didn't you hear me yelling stop? Look what you have done you pulled the fr---en pulley through the back of the barn and tore of some boards off the side of the barn." By then I was crying and telling him that I was worried about hitting the cows. He immediately calmed down and tried to calm me down. It had to be frustrating for dad to have a son that wanted nothing to do with farming and a drunkard for a brother that did not pull his weight and a wife that would rater be in a bar then at home helping on the family farm. Family farm! One man farm is more like it.

The days were OK together, there was no funny stuff or touching or anything it was as if nothing had ever happened. At times, I would convince myself that nothing happened but when bedtime came, I found myself returning to the closet to sleep and to feel safe but that did not work. Dad would feel around the bed-breathing heavy and calling my name in a raspy voice. He would ask why I was in the closet. I said nothing. Sometimes I would ask him to stop that and he would tell me it would be all right and that this was our secret, that mom did not have to know, as she would be mad at me. That was enough for me to keep my mouth shut, as I hated it when mom was mad at me. I was the peace keeper and I had to remember not to upset mom. Dad needed my help with the farm work as he could not afford to hire anyone to help.

Can I Go Along

Sometimes I would ask mom if I could go along when I felt more scared about being around Uncle Lewis and dad. Usually she would tell me she was not going anywhere. She would tell me it was nap time and I would beg her not to leave but that if she was going to go then I wanted to go. She would always sneak off when she thought I was sleeping. I would awake as soon as I heard the car start. Sometimes she would look up at the upstairs window and I would have my face pressed against the window screaming for her to wait for me but she never did. The child in me that I cry for is that child with her faced pressed against the window. If mom did take me I had strict orders to not go back and repeat to dad everything I heard or seen. If I did then I would not get to go again. That told me right there that what she was doing and saying would not have been approved by my dad. I do not have words to express how abandon I felt and how alone and unwanted I was.

On some occasions mom would drop me off at Grandma Cora's house to play with my cousins. Cora was really my aunt but I grew up calling her grandma with the rest of the kids and besides I did not have a grandma. I absolutely loved going there, as there was only her and three other girls, no men, no molestation, no disapproving looks, only a gentle smile that glowed with love and kindness. She would take all the time in the world to listen to the "babbling" of youth and seemed to find every word interesting. Her world was not that of makeup and fancy clothes and expensive perfume but her world of children, laughter, Spitz the dog and seeing her children was her wealth. A wealth that was there for others to share in as her door was always open.

Thanks mom! Thank you for not caring to spend time with me, thank you for dropping me off to be rid of me, to drive out of site and not look back. Thank you for not taking the time to even return and pick me up. I loved sleeping in a safe bed with little friends to play with. If I was lucky, I would have to stay three or four days before returning to home, a home cold and void of love, laughter, and happy times.

Grandma Cora's home was filled with love, laughter and the door was open all day long to the kids, the dog and the many flies that ran in and out with us. All that remains today are my vivid memories of that home, is the smell of the damp basement; the worn linoleum pattern on the floor where stood testimony to the miles covered by grandma's leg brace that she drug across the floor. The dragging sound I hear as fresh today as it was fifty years ago. The only fear I ever had there was looking at the teeth that stood in the glass near the kitchen sink. As a child, I wondered if they could jump out and bite me. She showed me what real love and acceptance was and I could have stayed and drank it in for the rest of my life. It is her memory that I have which I molded into my skills to mother my children. I know that I could never be half the person she was but I did learn the importance of time spent with my children and to listen to them.

Spinning Out of Control

Mom's drug addiction had become so bad. She was taking as many as thirty six pills a day and to the point of hallucinating. She did not know if she had been somewhere or if she had slept the day away. She literally lived in a drug-induced environment. Her world revolved around the pills, and to feel or rather not feel anything. She became more cold and clammy, and had a death look. I remember one time hiding her pills in the stairway as I hated what they did to her. I hated it that she gave them more attention than she did me. Why couldn't she just be happy with me instead of taking pills to become happy, a fake kind of happy? I would always put the pills back when I heard her turn into the driveway as she scared me with her wild looks and mean ways.

One time when we went into to Tyler to the drugstore, she told the owner of the place, that she needed more sleeping pills. He began to question her about it was rather soon to be wanting more pills; mom told him she had dropped them off her kitchen sink and they had dissolved in the sink. I looked up at her and said, "Mama you didn't drop any pills." In addition to that, I got a hard smack across the backside right there and told to hush up. The lesson that I learned and think about to this day is never tell a lie as I learned you get hit from telling the truth so what must happen to you if you lie!

She got more pills and was able to continue with this cycle of generated high's and ultimate lows. Some days she would sleep in bed all day only to get up and leave before dad was finished with night milk chores. Sometimes, she would be so glassy eyed and in a stupor, I do not see how she could really focus or drive in that shape. Sometimes she would have me drive her to Tyler at age 13 because she was so messed up. I was her friend and friend when she could get me to do this. She would drive the car out of the driveway so dad would not see that I was driving. Everybody threw me into an adult world a world that I should not have had to be a part of until it was time and on my terms.

One day she got up from a nap and said, "Let's go to town." So I got ready to go. We were less than 3 miles from home, in fact right in front of Karston's place when she was going 80 M. P. H. and cars were blowing their horns as she was in the middle of the road. Screaming at her to get over, "Why do you want to kill us please get back on your side of the road, please don't do this." She looked at me," Why not there is nothing to live for." I even tried to turn the wheel. I was so scared and wished that I had stayed home. We rolled right on through Lake Benton and on into Tyler. She stopped at the drugstore and played music boxes forever. Some songs made her cry and others made her happy. She eventually bought one. We drove home and she returned to bed crying herself to sleep. When she awoke, she came out into the living room, "Nanell get my cigarettes for me and an ashtray." As she sat there looking around with a glazed look in her eyes she started reaching out taking hold of something in mid air and turning her head from side to side. She kept plucking in the air. Finally, I asked her," What are you doing?" She replied, "I am picking spiders and apples. Don't you see them they are right there?" This really scared me, as there simply was nothing there. Eventually she quit and when she got up and walked through the dining room, she saw the music box sitting on the dining room table and wondered where that had come from and who got it. I said, "Mom don't you remember going into town to the drugstore and getting it?" She simply did not; she denied the fact that we had ever left the house. I questioned her about what happened by Karston's and she did not remember any of that.

The crying and confusion continued, and the pills kept going and going. Mom became more somber, listless, and harder to deal with. She did nothing for herself at this point, I was doing all the cooking and cleaning and laundry. She simply existed in her own world. Eventually it became necessary for her to enter the hospital in Minneapolis for drug addiction. By the time she did so she was taking more pills than ever along with a few drinks now and then. Based upon the calculations of the refills, they figure she was taking as many as thirty five pills a day. In Minneapolis they even did brain test to see if there was brain damage from all the pills and alcohol having been mixed. Ironically she never suffered brain damage. I often wondered if that machine could show how mentally ill she was if the reader part would have literally jumped off the charts!

Mom went back on the bus and was re-admitted to the hospital. Dave begged and begged to go see ma. I thought this was unusual. He only wanted to drive as he now had his driver's license, and he only wanted to hit mom up for money as he didn't care about mom, don't really know if he ever did for that matter. Anyway, I got to go along to Minneapolis and see her. We followed down dim lit hallways and the nurse brought out her keys and unlocked the door. I did not know that my mom was on a locked ward. I understood as soon as I seen her as she looked like she was lost and not aware of where she was. She trembled as she stuck out her hand to me. I could not touch her and I did not want to touch her and yet it tugged at my heart to see her looking such a mess. Mom always had every hair in place and the finest of clothing. Mom now lay in a wrinkled bed smelling of sweat and her hair was a mess a real mess. There above her bed was a long line of tongue depressors taped to the wall. The tongue depressors were there to be used if mom started to have seizures. It was quite common when a person was coming off drugs to have seizures. Mom looked like death warmed over. Mom always had her makeup on and I mean always! She would never wash it off at night but only after she would wake up in the mornings. She appeared very edgy and somewhat confused. She did not really seem glad to see us either. Dave started hitting her up for money right away and that was soon short lived as she began to cry and act confused. The nurse led us out to a day room filled with chairs, sun, and mentally ill patients. Some looked like raging killers to me and they just frightened me! While we waited for mom to come, the woman that sat before me took her wig off her head, she was bald, this was the first time I had even seen a wig! This was creepy to say the least. The woman began to comb her wig very calmly and place it back on her head.

When mom arrived and I told her about that she explained to me that the woman had seen her father commit suicide; she had a nervous breakdown and had lost all her hair from the shock of it. She talked about others and what was bothering them but not once did she talk about herself as far as the pills or her nerves. It was as if she was a visitor and all the rest had something wrong with them. We did not stay long as Dave was mad and wanted to leave once he found out she had no money. I may have only been thirteen but I did realize how wrong it was for Dave to be concerned about money.

I did realize that they were so much alike, both selfish, only out for what they wanted, not caring about what someone else may need or want. Sometimes mom was good to us but in a very sick kind of way. She never told us she loved us, not once just saying I love you. Love to her revolved around what we could do or give her but then the same was true for her friends. She would buy the world for a friend but if they did not do the same back then she would be pissed. Ultimately she was disappointed most of the time as others including her family could not fill her expectations.

Weekend Pass

Eventually the doctors felt that mom was good enough to come on the bus for a weekend to see how it would go. Dad would have to stop milking and run into town, pick her up at the bus station, then go back out, and finish milking. She just sat there smoking and not saying a word but I did notice she was swinging her leg just as fast as she could. Once again, she comes home and acting very different again.

The next night she decides to fix supper. Dave came up to the house and he started yelling at her for some reason. Soon she was yelling at him and I am begging, "Stop it both of you. There is no reason to fight, everything is OK." I stepped in between to keep Dave from hitting her. I was too scared to leave them alone and go to the barn and get dad. All at once mom turned around from the stove, "Who are you? I don't know you." She held the butcher knife up with a wild look in her eyes and said again, "Who are you? I don't know you." By this time that finally got Dave's attention and he told her, "It is me mom, your son, Dave." Mom steps toward us moving the knife and Dave yells, "You are crazy, what the hell is wrong with you?" All of a sudden, mom picks up a kettle that had silverware standing in it and threw it; I stepped in between and caught the kettle and silverware in the middle of my back. Dave grabbed the broom and pushed her into the corner pressing the broom across her throat trying to choke her. I couldn't pull him off and I could not get the broom away.

It was at this point I ran out the door screaming for dad to come to the house. He had just shut the milkers when he heard my yelling for him to come to the house. I explained everything that had happened, mom was crying and wanting to leave and that she did not belong here. Dad immediately called the hospital and it was set up for dad to drive her to Marshall and ride on the last bus there to go back to the hospital. Therefore, that is how the first weekend pass went. It was not right for her in her mental state to ride all the way to Minneapolis without someone sane with her, but then maybe none of us was sane! At the age of sixteen, Dave should have been knocked on his ass and told what to do and told to help instead of being able to try and run his mouth on mom and on me for that matter. He would rather fight than do anything helpful.

You Are Going to Be Crazy

Have you ever been told that you are going to be crazy? Just as crazy as your mother? Think about it from my eyes, I knew exactly how crazy she could be far better perhaps than anyone as everyone else in her life had places to go to escape the wrath of my mom but I did not. I received this phone call at 7:30 in the morning just before I got on the bus to go to school. She informed me that she had heard from a reliable source that mom was locked up in the mental ward and she was. Ever sit and wait for crazy to come, what would I do, how would I react? Would I grab my head like mom, would I look at others as strangers? Would I no longer know my mom, dad, or Dave? If I cried would that mean that I was going crazy? I stood frozen in my inner being to reach out, to talk, to move as I did not know what movement or sound would make me go crazy.

I think now that it is a miracle and a God send that I was not harmed worse. I am very lucky to have my wits about me and I have a good sense of humor and the ability to go outside myself and look back at myself with objectivity.

Meeting My First Boyfriend

Everyone around knew about the Showboat Ballroom east of Lake Benton and I honestly think everyone had probably been there at one time or another. The dance hall was located in a low half swampy area adjacent to the lake. If it rained at all, it was a sure bet that cars would be stuck.

My girlfriend, Terry, worked there every weekend with her family as they ran the place for the owner. She had begged me to come and I wanted to go. After lectures and accusations of why I really wanted to go, I left. Terry worked in the coat check and that suited me fine, as I was scared of crowds and people. I loved feeling safe behind the counter and being able to see cute boys come in and I enjoyed hearing the music.

The scariest thing for me was to walk the length of the dance floor to the bathrooms on the other end of the dance hall. I had no one to walk across the hall with, as we had to have one person in the coat check area at all times. I worried that a boy might grab or touch me. After all, after being so sexually abused for years that is what you automatically think when you see a strange face is that they want to abuse you. If a familiar face will bring harm to you, then surely, a stranger would do the same. I was so shy that I could not even look anyone in the eye.

A few times guys asked me to dance and I would politely say no thank you while all the time on the inside wishing I could say yes. I just did not trust anyone or anything. Finally, when this boy asked me to dance Terry told me to go and opened the door all the while laughing, as she knew I was scared but of course she did not know the reason why. I was so self-conscious and scared to have eye contact and yet he smelled good. As we danced, we at least exchanged names and I learned his name was Gradin. We danced a few times and then the slow dance came and I left the floor. I did not want to but I was too scared to stay and dance.

Gradin came up and talked to me at the coat check and we exchanged small talk, in the end, he got me to go out and slow dance with him. It felt awkward, nice, and frightening all at the same time. He held my hand as we left the dance floor. We shared our phone numbers and hoped to see each other again on the following Saturday. He called me the next day and he wanted my address. When I got off the phone mom said, "I suppose you screwed him didn't you? You better not let me find out what you did Nanell or you will not go anywhere again." I hated that talk coming from her as she made me sound dirty, she did not know who I was as a person. She was too busy being immoral to even know the status of my morals.

God forbid that I should utter a word of that where she could hear. I thought of her as a dirty woman. I resented the fact that she had more smiles and laughter with her friends then she did with her family. We were not the center of her world; instead, we were on the edge of her world. It didn't matter what I said I did or didn't do she already had her mind made up and if I appeared to be happy then she handed out the threat that I probably wouldn't be allowed to ever go out there again and I certainly wasn't allowed to date and crawl around the back seat of a car. I know now that is what she no doubt did.

I lived for Gradin's letters and longed to see him. His letters were filled with kind words, the kind words that I had longed for all my life. Like you are pretty, you are nice, and cannot wait to see you. I was almost certain that I had to be in love and he must love me to talk so nice to me. Saturday night came and I was not allowed to go. The neighbor lady had called and wanted me to baby sit and mom accepted on my behalf before even asking me. I know now that she did it out of pure meanness. I was heartbroken and figured for sure that Gradin would find someone else. After all, who would want me?

Miserable People Live to Make Others Miserable!

That Sunday Gradin called and asked for directions to the house as his friend would drive him over. I was as excited and scared as I had no idea how my mom would act. When I told her, she informed me that I was not leaving the yard. Then she got dad involved telling him I had already been with a boy the first damn time I go out there now they are coming out here. I explained to dad how we met and that I had only danced with him, talked to him on the phone, and exchanged letters.

Gradin showed up with Rocky his best friend. Rocky was big and jolly and giggled a lot. Gradin was glad to see me and hugged me. I was in awe and nervous. They had their fishing poles with them and wanted to know if there was a place where the fish were biting; and could I go along fishing? I ran into the house begging to go and dad said he did not know these boys and mom was saying, "Nanell I know what you are going to do. They want to more than fish with you." I was so mad but I knew if I showed my temper I would not go anywhere.

Finally, dad agreed to come out and meet them, they offered for him to go fishing as well. My dad loved to fish but could not go as it was almost chore time but I think the invitation eased his mind. He suggested the Arco Park and that I could show them how to get there. I never said a word but that was the last place I wanted to be as that is where Weston would take me and molest me.

We laughed and talked all the way to Arco. As we pulled in the park, I felt myself feeling queasy with the thoughts and memories of the smell and breathing. I glanced around just to make sure that it was safe there and that Weston was not there. Rocky parked the car in the exact same spot Weston had parked us. All these feelings, fears, and thoughts and I could not say a word. The thoughts never went away and I could not wait to leave. We did catch a few bullheads and returned to the farm to clean them and fry them up for dad and all of us. By the time we did this, my dad was fine with Rocky and Gradin both.

Mom was actually nice to them, she talked and laughed with them and spoke nice to me like we were the best of friends. Rocky and Gradin thought she was nice and a fun person. Ya right! If they only knew what she was like but if I were to say that, I would look like the bad one. She was flirting with them the whole time they were there and they could not see it but I knew she was as that was what she was all about with any male person. She lived for trying to get the attention of other men.

If mom was down and out or had an argument with one of her guy friends, I bared the brunt of it. She would tell me I couldn't go out just to be mean. If she wanted to run with a man then it was OK for me to go out on a date. When she was miserable she spread it like soft butter on me.

Gradin and I became serious and he told me I was his girl, no one else. For the first time I found someone that really loved me and wanted me to belong to him. I lived for his every minute. Sometimes he would even cry and say it had been along week and longed to see me again. He could not imagine life without me. This had to be love.

We spent the summer fishing and going to the showboat dancing. I also learned the taste of slow gin, and how it could make you feel. When I drank it, I giggled a lot and was happy. I also let my guard down and allowed him to make love to me. It was awful as all I could hear in the dark was the heavy breathing, which reminded me of dad, Uncle Lewis, and Weston. I just wanted it to end. It just seemed to me that each time anyone touched me I really thought everyone could just tell by looking at me that they would know what I had done.

Eventually I noticed Gradin was smiling at other girls sometimes talking to them. I felt so scared that I would lose him. I did not know them and they would look over at me and grin. I thought for sure they were talking about me. Maybe they knew what others had done to me. Maybe he was telling them and they were laughing about it. Eventually I learned that they were girls from his class and they were asking him about me. I met them and I listened to them talk. I was not comfortable with them or was it that I was not comfortable with Gradin looking at them and not at me. Whatever the reason I did not like it. He knew I was bothered and laughed at me thought it was cute that it did bother me.

More and more when we did go to the dance hall he would leave me sit and go visit with others and even dance with other girls from time to time. I let my mood show and wore my heart on my sleeve. He clearly knew he had me and that I was not going anywhere. After all, who would have me? I had better be glad that I had him. Besides, I had met his family and enjoyed my time with them. I loved his mom she was nice and talked nice to me.

One time we went to a party at one of his friend's house, her parents were gone, we all crowded into their basement, and someone said they had brought a movie along. There must have been 10 or 12 people and everyone packed on couches and chairs and on the floor. To my utter surprise, someone had put in a porn movie. I only knew that it was one because it started out by saying it was. I could have died, I felt sick, the room became quiet as everyone starred at the movie and some snuggled closer. It was a most horrible time for me; I was so embarrassed and uncomfortable. It was even more uncomfortable when the lights came on and we all starred at each other. No one said a word and we all left soon after.

Gradin knew about my mom seeing other men as his dad frequented the bars and had seen my mom there with other men. I was so upset and ashamed. I did not want Gradin's dad to think that I approved of it or that I was like her in any way. I cried and told him that I had a hard time getting along with my mom and that she was never there. Gradin learned to flirt with mom in order to get around her bad mood and get me out of the house. I still resented the fact that she flirted back and I resented it that he flirted with her. I did not feel I could compete with my mother or anyone else for that matter as I could not flirt. As for the rest of my past, I could not utter one word. If you talk like that and share ugliness like that then others will think you want to do it and like it.

After about a year of going together and experiencing having feelings for a person, feelings that I wanted to have and not the feelings of someone I did not want touching me, I began to experience severe pain in my left side. It hurt so bad that I could not stand up. Mom reluctantly took me to the doctor, I say reluctantly because my having to go to the doctor messed up her plans to go to the bar with Elsie. Elsie was her lady friend that ran the bars with her. While they were friends I think also they were at times in competition for the same man.

Tubal Pregnancy

Upon completion of my exam, Dr. Bob informed my mom that I had a tubal pregnancy, that if the fetus did not expel on its own it could cause my tube to rupture, and they maybe would have to go in surgically to repair and or remove the fetus. He figured it would expel on its own and that was a part of the pain I was experiencing.

Mom looked like the cat that swallowed the canary. She seemed pleased and angry all at the same time. Dr. Bob talked to her and me about being on birth control pills once I got this behind me. He then left us alone to talk it over. What was there to talk about! Mom started in by calling me a whore, a tramp, and saying I was no good and what would your dad think! For the first time I said what about what you do with Willard and those other men at the Florence bar. I was scared and I was hurting.

It was at that point we locked eyes and informed me that I was not going out with Gradin anytime soon and that maybe she would have to tell his parents about all this. She then had a gleam in her eyes as she said to me, "I will let you get the birth control pills as long as you don't tell dad about what you see or hear when you are with me." BLACK MAIL pure and simple! I agreed and then she said, "This does not mean that you lay on your back every chance you get!"

At sixteen years old, I felt all the rebellion. I resented her for what she did, what she stood for, and the way she liked to make me look dirty. What I felt in my heart was not dirty. Others were dirty, others made me keep secrets and now she was too. I had secrets about dad, Weston, Uncle

Lewis, now mom and her affairs. Whom could I turn to with all my secrets? Who cared? I felt awful agreeing to keep a secret from dad. I know it was wrong and nothing made it right but mom had no right to even make me promise such a thing. I wonder how many other children ever had this many secrets or this kind of screwed up life? It is no wonder that I felt like a freak that did not belong anywhere. I am not like other people and today I cherish that.

One Secret Fell Out of the Web

Mom became more and more brazen, I hated her and I hated myself. If dad only knew what was going on. What would he think of me being on the pill? Even though things had changed somewhat, I still did not want to have any kind of talk with him about anything pertaining to sex. I still hated the nights still feared that he would try to come upstairs. I didn't want him to know I wore a bra and I didn't want him to know I had periods.

On this particular day when I got home from school, I grabbed the cards to have our usual game of cribbage before we went out to do feeding chores. As I shuffled the cards he turned and looked at me and said "Not tonight I have to hurry with chores as we are going out tonight." when I asked him who was taking them out to eat, he said, "Willard, It is his way of thanking mom for helping with thank you notes on the death of his wife." Mom and Elsie or maybe not Elsie, had gone over to Willard's and helped write the thank you notes after she had died and so that was his excuse to take them out to eat. I knew in my heart of hearts that Willard really only wanted to take mom out and I knew that that was the last thing my dad wanted to do as he never went anywhere.

This could not be happening I thought and I could not sit here and let it happen and yet if I told on mom I would have to tell on myself first. I must tell and get all this off my chest no matter what. "Dad I have something to tell you, you can't go out with mom and Willard you just can't." We sat by the kitchen table, he at one corner of the table and I at the other corner. I started itching all over and began to develop red welts on my arms and legs. I felt so shaky and had such a dry mouth I could hardly get any words to come out. Immediately began to cry and talk at the same time. The floor beneath me was the only thing I could look at. I began to tell him of having slept with Gradin and having gone through a tubular pregnancy and how Dr. Bob thought that mom and I should talk about being on birth control pills.

Dad bit down on his pipe and made a swirling motion with his hands as he rubbed one inside the other. He gently said, "I would rather you be on the pill than a child with a child. Thank you for telling me." It was at this point that I knew I had to tell him the rest but I was frightened of what he might do or say and I was scared to death of what mom might do.

As all the ugliness of mom and her affair with Willard and my knowledge of it slid from the deepest part of my heart with all kinds of emotions. I glanced at dad and told him how she black mailed me with the birth control pills and how I could no longer keep all this to myself and I could not let that ugly man take dad anywhere.

Dad sounded choked up and asked me if Elsie knew that this had been going on and I nodded my head that yes she knew. Quietly he told me he loved me, which is the first time that he ever said the words to me. He then proceeded to bend over and tie his shoes, his pipe trembled between the five remaining teeth he had. As he grabbed the doorknob, he told me to send mom up to the barn when she got home and that I should stay in the house. Now I was scared, after all, I had never really seen my dad angry about anything and what was he thinking. Was he going to hurt her, kill her, kill him and her, kill himself? I just did not know what mom would say. He never asked her to come up to the barn unless it was to show her a new baby calf and even then, she did not want to go.

What would mom do to me? What would happen with their little plan to go out tonight? Would dad still go out and pretend nothing was wrong; would he maybe go and then kill them both? All I could do was listen for her returning car and feel sick to my stomach. The questions came fast and furious without any answers to them. Suddenly I heard the car door shut, she was within five feet of looking me in the eye. Gosh, I was scared. Scared of the unknown as nothing like this had ever happened to me before. She was going to be in for the shock of her life, a shock that I had created but not really as it was all of her wrong doing coming to a head. I also felt better about not keeping a secret from my dad.

Mom came through the door looking at me bewildered and wondering why I was not helping dad with feeding chores as they had plans to go out this evening. I met her gaze feeling scared but yet in control for now even if it was just for a second, I had something on her, and the tables had changed. I told her that dad was in the barn and that he wanted to see her up there when she got back

I felt as though I was transparent and that she knew I had told. My heart was racing, as I was scared of what might happen. She looked at me and asked if we had a new calf up in the barn and if that was what dad wanted to show her.

As the kitchen door shut behind her, I quickly ran to the kitchen window feeling as though my heart was in my mouth. What was going to happen! Would dad finally snap and kill her. Would he kill himself! What had I gone and done and how was I going to deal with mom. As she entered through the milk house door, I quickly ran up to the barn and peeked through the small west door.

There stood dad and mom face to face. Dad asked her, "Where have you been and who have you been with?" When she replied Elsie, dad asked her if that was a lie. She looked scared really scared for the first time. Dad then held out his hands for the car keys and asked her for them. She said they were in the house and dad told her to leave them on the kitchen table and that she was to call Willard and tell him that they would not be going out to eat not now, not ever. In his calm manner, he told her that she was his wife and that if she wanted to stay there would be no more seeing Willard.

First words out of her mouth were "Did that no good Nanell tell you, who said anything about Willard, I suppose it was her." Dad informed her that it did not matter who said what but that it was going to stop right now or she could leave. Upon hearing that I headed for the house, I really realized what I had done and that there was no way that mom was not going to raise seven kinds of hell with me.

When I got into the kitchen, I quickly ran for the bathroom and locked the door shut behind me. No sooner had I done that than mom came through the kitchen door slamming it just as hard as she could. "Nanell you little son of a bitch you had better get your ass out here right now. I am not fooling. You and I will talk sooner or later." She then banged on the bathroom door yelling at me and I stood frozen with ears ringing and heart pounding. Eventually she made her way to the phone and called Elsie and Willard. She was mad and crying.

I knew I had to come out of the bathroom eventually as I had to baby sit for the neighbor lady and she would soon be here to pick me up. Just as soon as I got out the bathroom door, she got in my face. At first I said nothing but she wouldn't leave me alone so I got my coat on and was planning to walk up to the neighbors to baby sit when she yelled, "Just where the hell do you think you are going? If I cannot go anywhere, you need not think that you can. You little son of a bitch! Why did you tell, just wait until I tell your dad about you being on birth control pills. What do you think he will think of his precious daughter then...?" I headed out the door and she informed me I better get my ass back inside and I was not about to go out with Gradin.

She grabbed my arm and I spun around full of anger and fear," You are a whore! Who said I was going out with Gradin? I have a babysitting job tonight." She slapped me across the face so hard I wanted to cry but instead I looked her in the eye and said," Do it again if it makes you feel better," and by God she did it again!

If I was to ever be anywhere with her after that she was quick to say, "Be careful what you say in front of Nanell she will run home and tell her dad." They would just look at me with disapproving eyes but those eyes were not anymore disapproving then mine were right back at them. There I stood in the midst of the lowest, they were looking to judge me? They that did not know just how mean, and selfish my mother was, the selfishness they could not see because they were only thinking of their own selfish gains from her. I felt that my mother was a whore, a liar, and a cheat. She was lazy, worthless, and mean. I only felt that she used her mental illness as a weapon to hold us at bay, to release her from any accountability or obligation of her actions or the lack there of.

High School Prom

Overall school, work, family life and having a feel for leaving home working towards a goal were absolutely nothing to do with my thinking process. My live consisted more of daily survival from all the abuse. There were no words of encouragement, no hugs; no I love you, no looks of appreciation, no reassurance of any kind. No wonder I suffered low self-esteem.

Even as I looked to my first prom and having a dress made just for me, mom would say, "better make sure the zipper works as you won't keep it on, and you better not come home knocked up." She could make you feel so cheap and dirty on top of me already feeling dirty from my dad, uncle, and cousin. All of which she did not know anything about.

We had our prom and others take pictures as my parents never bothered to come up to the school to take pictures or watch as we marched in. We stayed at the prom until eleven or so then we went to his parents and changed clothes, we met up with other kids, had a bonfire out in a field, and had some beer. Around five, that morning we went and dug worms and some of us went fishing until noon. Upon returning home and showing our catch of fish mom made sure to sneak her remarks of, "I bet you didn't fish all night, I bet that isn't all you did." It was awful how she could make a person feel. She could make you crawl inside your own skin with fear and shame.

That summer I saved all the money I could working as a carhop at the drive inn in Lake Benton, as mom and dad's twenty fifth wedding anniversary was coming soon and I wanted to give them something special, something that would make them happy. Finally, when the day came near, I bought dad a grinder so he would be able to sharpen his own sickle blades and that would save him time and money. Gradin and I got it set up in the shop and waited until dad was through milking to show him. He seemed genuinely touched by it.

Gradin left as he had to get home. As dad and I walked down through the yard towards the house I told him there was one more surprise and as he opened the entry door he seen our broken down kitchen table in the entry way, and in the kitchen stood the brand new chrome kitchen table with four chairs. He said that it was nice of me to do that but that I should not have spent all my money on them. We went in the living room and visited. Soon mom drove in, I immediately jumped up realizing that I had not done up the dirty dishes. Dad told me not to worry and that she would understand once she seen what I had done. Well mom came through the door and without turning on the kitchen light, she started yelling for me to get those G– damn dishes done. Dad immediately told her to shut up and turn the kitchen light on

She then did a 180-degree turn and began to act nice. She also asked immediately how much I had paid for it and I told her she should not ask that. I immediately did the dishes and headed to bed heartbroken. All the way upstairs, I sobbed and wondered if I would ever make her happy or proud of me. She did not care about their anniversary or being at home.

My Future

What was I going to do after school? I was not smart enough to learn anything. I had thought about going up to the cities and being a housekeeper for money, as I sure knew how to do that and to baby sit. The thought of that frightened me as I could not see me being that far away from home and I sure could not drive up in the cities. I finally signed up for beauty school at Austin Minnesota but I knew that I could never pass that and I did not know where I would live or how I would pay the rent.

Gradin had already been out a year and was completing his year of training at the welding school in Canby. We decided to get married and that sure sounded like a life saver to me as I did not know what I could do. All I knew was I wanted to leave home and get as far away from mom as I could. I knew I loved Gradin and I would be faithful and kind to him and I would gladly keep his house and cook his meals.

One month to the day, after graduating from high school, Gradin and I were married on June 28 1969. After nearly 2 and ½ years of going together, we thought we were ready for marriage. I loved his family and especially his mom. She was a thousand times more the mom than I ever had.

Surely Gradin loved me, after all, he called, he came over, he cried and if he were a little mean, he would say that he was sorry. No one had ever said sorry to me before. All I knew was that I loved him and I wanted to be all that he would ever need out of life. For me love was not about shiny objects it was about being together, being kind to each other a team that no one could beat or tear apart.

Gradin bought my white knee length dress for ten dollars and was so proud of how cheap he got it. I did not dare tell him that I did not like the vinyl belt with it. He had gotten my wedding band and was even more proud that it only cost him four dollars. The marriage license was ten dollars, the wedding dress was ten dollars, and the ring was four dollars. Twenty-four dollars and I thought it was an investment in our future, our desire to become one, to live happily ever after.

The night before the wedding, we had rehearsal at the Catholic Church in Tyler; it was there that I had taken instruction to turn Catholic for my husband to be. Kelli and Rocky were standing up for us; they too were engaged although Kelli did not seem to be enthusiastic about it though. Kelli and I figured we would hang out with the guys after rehearsal but that was not what they had planned. Gradin was short and snappy with me, I started to cry right away, and that only made him mad. They got in Gradin's car and squalled tires as they left. My heart was broken and I didn't know if I wanted to go through with tomorrow or not but right behind that thought I also didn't know what I would do if I didn't go through with it. After all the invitations were mailed, I could not back out now.

Kelli and I drove over to Lake Benton to the Drive Inn where I had worked and went inside. We decided to have a hamburger and fries. We were both quiet I guess mainly because I was in such a bad mood. Soon the telephone rang there and it was for me, it was my mother informing me to get my ass home as I was not married yet, and I was not 18 yet. It was almost 10:00 p. m. at night and the night before my wedding. What was I doing so terrible! I was brought back to reality by her sharp voice yelling, "You get your ass home now."

The minute I did get home, she started in on me. I ran upstairs to be safe from her, as she never came upstairs more than three times in all my years of living there. Sleep was the only way to escape her mouth. The next morning I awoke to the sound of rain and thunder. Kelli and I were going to meet at the church to set out the daisies from her mom's garden. There was no money for flowers and fancy invitations.

As mom and dad drove me to the church she started in about I had better put that belt on with that dress. I informed her that it was my wedding and I was not wearing it. At this point, I could not even feel excited about getting married as Gradin, I had a fight last night, and he never bothered to call me and say he was sorry or never called to tell me he loved me. I could not back out now because the wedding would start within an hour and all the people not that many on my side but on Gradin's side, besides his mother liked me and did not want to lose that. Mom D had already taught me a lot and she had toughness about her that I liked and wished I had.

As I looked out the car window the rain poured down harder and harder, we were close to the church, and mom was still bitching. I do not know how dad put up with it all these years but even now, dad was of no support to me as he usually took the role of silence when she was in her hateful moods. We did make eye contact in the rear view mirror we neither had to say a word. I learned that look a long time ago and that look meant for me to shut up and not upset mom. Oh well none of this will matter once I am in Gradin's arms. Upon arrival at the church Gradin came around the corner and glared at me and oh how that hurt. If he could only see in my heart all the love I had for him, he would never look at me like that. Just then he told me all the flowers were dead, not one single daisy made it then he started to laugh. I wanted to die! I should have known the marriage was doomed with the rainy cloudy day, dead flowers; he could not even look at me with kindness, not a wedding picture was taken, cheap dress and ring. Not everything a girl dreams about was happening here at all. Five minutes at the altar and our journey together was about to begin. Why did I feel scared and worried about if he even was happy or wanted me to be his wife?

After the ceremony, a small group of us went to the neighboring town of Arco for a little lunch before Gradin and I left for a northern Minnesota fishing resort. Oh how exciting to get away and go fishing, and yet I remember feeling scared to go that far away with him all alone. We drove what seemed like hours before arriving at the place. Gradin had to show them our marriage certificate as they thought we were too young to be renting a room. This of course made him mad.

(The hardest part in writing this is about the sexual encounters. I am not afraid to relive this account but rather what bothers me is wanting to make sure that I can portray the distinction between a sexual act and lovemaking)

I view love making as a mutual agreed upon union between two people wanting to please and enjoy each other, a gift to share and explore together. Sex is a cold and calculated set of moves that only satisfies the perpetrator and leaves physical and emotional scars on the victim and in the darkest hours of night the difference between the two kinds of activity become the checks and balances between sanity and insanity.

To this day I remember each and everyone that touched me and at my youngest and most tender age of childhood and marriage I was raped so many times.

Honeymoon Night

Nervously I stepped out of the shower; I was excited, as this would be my first time with my very own husband. I slid into the blue nightee I had bought and could not wait to see if he looked at me with approving eyes. He was behind the bathroom door waiting for me, as he grabbed me I stumbled and he threw me onto the bed, tore my nightee off, it was there in the dark of the night I became his property to have and to hold and use anyway he wanted to from that day forward. As he slept, I cried silently in the dark wondering if it was always going to be this way, painful and like I did not matter. The next morning I awoke to him standing over me taking his clothes off. Not once did he ask me if I wanted to or did he try to put me in a loving mood. All I know is that I was very sore from the night before and it hurt and I could not wait for it to be done, the deed, the act, the ugliness of man to be done. I was informed that there would be no more nice nighties, I could sleep naked, and there would be no more crying as only babies cry.

Our First Home

In June of 1969, we settled into our first home in Madison. It was there that Gradin went to work for Mark's Manufacturing and I stayed at home for the first week. I enjoyed being all alone and settling into our home, it was important for me to keep it cleaned, to have his food cooked and his clothes washed. I wanted to be perfect for him. Our home consisted of living on the middle floor of a three-story house. Below lived a married couple and upstairs above us lived two single school teachers that were females. The stairs that led to their apartment was right outside our bedroom door. Gradin loved to tell me when he could hear them come in that he bet they wanted him to screw them and he imagined them walking up the steps with no panties on, and how beautiful they must be. He did and said anything to make me feel inferior, inferiority that I already felt before he ever came into my life. I just longed for someone to love me and appreciate me, it did not matter that I did not love myself. I figured all I had to do is love others and I would be OK, I did not matter only others mattered. I started feeling anxious about the time he was to come home from work. I never knew if he was going to be in a good mood, tired, or glad to see me.

My First Beating

When he got home, I started telling him about having called dad and talked to him and that dad said to tell him hello. Gradin immediately looked mean as hell at me and asked me who gave me permission to call home. I was not allowed to call home anymore and he let me know that he paid the bills around there and he would be checking the phone bill when it came in to make sure that I had not called. I gently asked him if we could go home this weekend and see him, as we had not yet gone home since we had got married. That really pissed him off and he shoved me towards the bed and lay out the rules of his house. 1. There would be no more phone calls. 2. No crying. 3. No asking to see my parents ever. 4. If I tried to leave he would get me for stealing the car as it was in his name and he would be checking the mileage. If I needed money, I was to ask him and then I had to show a receipt for every dollar I spent and show the change, as he did not want me keeping anything for myself. I was to keep to myself and not talk to others about him. That night after going to bed and I thought he was sleeping I was crying when all of a sudden he reached out and touched me. I was horrified as I knew he was serious.

Gradin jumped out of bed and grabbed a metal coat hanger the heavy thick kind and doubled it up, he then turned me belly down and straddled me. He then commenced to beating me repeatedly raising welts on my back, it hurt so badly and when I started to cry, he said he would continue to beat me until I stopped and I was to beg him to stop.

He then ripped my panties down around my knees and lay down on me jabbing me repeatedly, it hurt so bad and he held the back of my neck into the bed almost choking off my breathing. When he was done I asked his permission to go to the bathroom, it was there that I realized I was bleeding rectally as well as vaginally I hurt all over and my back was fire engine red and swollen some areas were turning bluish purple.

The only lesson I learned from this beating was to never let any son of a bitch get behind me ever again. My back was sore, my butt was sore and my bottom hurt. I felt so alone and so frightened and I knew I had no way out. Perhaps this would not happen again and I could keep him from getting so mad at me. Each day I grew more quiet and afraid of Gradin or afraid at least of what I knew he was capable of doing. I was a failure at marriage, as I could not make him happy. I know now that I had not failed him. He was a sick failure before I ever came along.

Get PG and Get a Job

Gradin was worried about being drafted and having to go off to Vietnam. He kidded with his friends that he would go to Canada. I knew he was not kidding though as he did not want to go off to war. He had heard that he could drop blood drops in his urine sample and that would keep him from going. That would give him a classification of 4F and that is what he needed to be rejected by the military. In addition, if I were PG this would give him some kind of delay, and so it became my duty to get PG or he would be going to Canada and without me.

He wanted me to get a job and that literally frightened me, as I did not know how to ask for a job as any place I had worked they had sought me out. He took the morning off and told me to be ready to get a job that he would take me down to the local cafe, and I had better get a job. The only restaurant I went into was not hiring at the time. I was so nervous that when I got home I puked and lost my guts. I was so sick and frightened. He told me to be ready tomorrow to go look for a job and to give him a list of places I tried and that he would check and see if I had actually gone and applied.

My life was saved! Early the next morning the cafe across the street had called as the other cafe let them know that I was looking for work. I just felt different as they were asking me I did not feel like I was begging. Gradin had not mentioned this cafe even though he stopped there every morning for his 10:00 a. m. coffee break. I did not understand why he did not want me to work there. I figured it out when I arrived as there was a pretty waitress that he liked to flirt with, I know as he did it in front of me.

The La Que Parole hotel and cafe was where I got my first job. The elderly lived in the hotel part and it was their last stop before the nursing home. I would have to be a morning short order cook and that he knew I could handle it. He said the residents ordered the same thing morning after morning. I learned to start cooking for them as I seen them come across the lobby floor, oatmeal and toast, 2 scrambled eggs, cold cereal, toast and coffee all of which was very simple and they didn't mind waiting as there was nothing else going on in their day until the next meal came around. Having the elderly for regular kind and loving people made me feel more secure about my cooking and about my job.

I hadn't been there a week when on a Saturday morning I and the cook opened, Polly went right to work to fix the noon meal and I immediately turned the grill on up front in anticipation of the usual. All of a sudden the front door opened and eight railroad men walked in, they were wet, hungry and it was I who had to serve them.

Lord my stomach turned, I could not imagine cooking for them. I put my game face smile on to try to hide my fear. After placing their water glasses in front of them and handing them the menu, I told them that I would return to take their order. Truth is I wanted to bolt out the front door and not look back but I could not do that.

With pen and pad, I approached the table thinking that maybe this would be something easy, they were kind and were kidding me. I love to kid so that did put me at ease a little. It did not take me long to lose any easiness I felt as they were ordering steak! Steak medium rare, steak well done, steak rare, and double orders of hash browns, double orders of toast! I did not even know where the steak was kept let alone all the variations in cooking; all I had ever done was fry hamburgers and deep fry French fries. I had only been here a week and here I was fixing all this and my regulars were starting to trail in. I had the place all to myself except for Polly working on the noon menu in the back.

I wanted to just cry but I did not as there was not time. I cooked what I thought was a double order of hash browns; it could have been a triple serving for all I know. Plate after plate I delivered their food and with a smile I told them if anything was not as they had hoped to just let me know that I would be more than happy to make it right. Well two steaks had to be returned to the grill, which I got them the way they wanted and I kept the coffee coming. I was determined that I was going to get through this if nothing else on politeness and full cups of coffee. Much to my pleasure things went fine and I even got a nice tip. (Now remember that was in 1969) I was happy to get a total tip of $2.00 from all of them.

After they left I immediately took a bathroom break! Nervous stomach was something that I had been born with. I always had to watch what I ate and to not get too upset as I would only end up in the bathroom. It made it hard to enjoy anything but then perhaps I hadn't enjoyed anything yet.

Turn Over the Money

One of the rules I learned was on payday. I was so proud of my check but I mostly hoped that I was pleasing Gradin as that was more important than anything. I must remember if he is happy I will be OK. I jumped in front of him holding my check in front of my face in hopes that he would be as pleased as I was. He looked at me with such contempt in his eyes almost as if he hated me and I didn't understand why. He immediately handed me a pen and said, "sign it." He then took it and put it in his billfold. Gradin held his hand out and wanted all tips that I had gotten and I was warned that I had better not lie about it.

If I needed to get groceries I had to account for every penny and I was not to buy myself anything without his permission, which meant no. When I drove down to the local laundry mat I was to stop by where he worked and let him know where I was going and show him the money I was using for the wash. I had to be home in time for supper and supper was to be on the table at 6P. M. sharp! In other words if I wasn't finished with the laundry I was to leave it there and run home and get supper started and also stop in and let him know.

Years after this marriage ended, I still could not throw away leftovers or keep left over food without getting my husband to tell me what he wanted me to do with them. When he would laugh and say he didn't care, I felt he was setting me up for a beating. I often think that Gradin left me more crippled than a person in a wheel chair. Learning to do and think and make decisions and having positive outcomes from doing so was the start of my healing. My kid's have laughed at me because it has taken me years to learn to put butter in the fridge. I took a few ugly beatings because the butter was not soft enough to spread.

Staying Out of the Way

Quickly I learned to stay out of his way and to not bother him and it would go better. I would take my time doing dishes as he didn't want me to sit near him in the living room while he drank beer and watched TV. He wasn't 21 yet but he had someone buying it for him. When he yelled for anything I was to bring it to him immediately no matter what I was doing.

Many times I would catch him picking his nose and eating it, he would offer me some and I politely said no. He would laugh and tell me that it was good and it gave him white corpuscles. He wouldn't brush his teeth. All this going on and I had no say, and no rights; yet he never failed to mention that I should worship him and that I was fat and should do something about it. I only weighed 105 when we got married and I was losing weight.

Often times he would stare at other women and point out how beautiful they were and he bet they would be good in bed. He never once said I looked nice or said thank you for anything I did. No since in complaining as I had no money, no car, and couldn't make phone calls. I had to report in to him with every move. If I did dwell on how I felt it didn't take long to realize that I was a complete failure at everything. I wasn't the daughter mom wanted; I wasn't the wife Gradin wanted. I was just plain worthless and in addition, all alone to live like this. I certainly knew there was no going home as I could hear now my mom asking me what had I done wrong this time or you made your bed now lie in it or I told you so. There for sure would be no concern for me. I did call my dad collect a couple times and made excuses that he didn't want me running up a phone bill but deep down I think my dad knew, at least wise in the end he definitely knew what I had gone through. I quit calling dad as I knew this was more money for him to pay out on bills and I knew he didn't have extra to spend on me besides what was there to talk about except that Gradin was getting meaner and more demanding and I was unable to please him it seemed.

Baby

Sick again! I just hadn't been feeling good. Smells odors and tastes were making me feel awful. I could be PG as I had quit taking the pill when he told me to and he would even get mad when I got my period as he wanted me PG so he wouldn't have to go into the army and off to war.

Perhaps I had done something right but I learned long ago not to get my hopes up as I was as irregular as they come with getting my period. Finally I told him I thought I was PG and he did allow me to go to the doctor and find out and yes I was. He seemed happy and all I could think about is how happy we would be as a family and that I wanted to give him a son, which I figured, would please him. Our world was not about having a baby but it was all about him and what he wanted which meant if he wanted rough sex then he took it.

There was no concern about how I was feeling and that I had better be ready to have sex with him anytime he wanted it. I hated the word sex as that to me was cold and lifeless without feeling but then again maybe sex was the right word for this "relationship" we had. While I had the thoughts of a new baby and all excited because I had done something right that he wanted me too, I did notice that he didn't seem to be enthusiastic about the coming of a child. One night while he was having sex with me he told me that he hoped that I had a girl as he would want to be the first to have sex with it, to teach it right about what a man could do. I was just horrified at the thought and sickened to no end as I knew what a "man" could do to a child. I didn't understand why he talked so hateful about his own flesh and blood.

107

The night before I lost the baby he lashed out at me," It is probably the baby of some nigger, and it will be a black baby. Besides if it is a girl I will be the first to screw it. That will by my job." First off, I never entertained the thought of cheating on him as that would be a death sentence for sure and secondly there was not one I repeat not one black person within probably 100 miles of Madison. Here I was alone in another one of his many sick traps that he had in his head. All his sick traps were out of sight in his head but they had the teeth of steel that held my head and heart in a jail that was invisible to the outside world.

He left for work in the morning without any more pleasantry than the day before or the day before that. He was gone and I had a couple hours before I had to be to work at the cafe up town. I quickly put on some music and turned it up just a little to tune out life as it existed. Quickly I cleaned and picked up around the house in hopes to eliminate any beatings that night. Now I finally had time just for me and I wanted a nice hot bath and to be able to soak out all the fears and twists that life had offered me in this short time we had been married. My baby and I would soak up the softness of a bubble bath and I would enclose myself with the love that every mother feels for her first unborn child with all the hopes and dreams of a blessed life and the cherished gift that lay as a small knot in my belly.

I knew it was useless to soak as in a few minutes I would again smell more like the kitchen at the cafe than a fresh bar of soap. The bath was an escape like nothing else and it gave me the strength to smile again, have hopes again, and to dream again about what beauty was yet to come.

I stood in front of the mirror combing my black hair and feeling back to the reality of not seeing anything-pretty look back at me. I studied my teeth tried to make sure that every pimple was covered. I hated them and had fought them since I was 9 years old. It didn't matter what I did or what I did not do they were always there and that was all I could see. I checked my makeup and studied my uniform to make sure there were no wrinkles when all of a sudden the door flew open and there before me stood Gradin with that wild hateful look in his eyes. I smiled and said, "Hi honey." He jerked me up and said, "I suppose you have been out fu--ing again haven't you?" He went on about how when he went for his 10:00 coffee break I wasn't there and everyone wondered where I was and that I wasn't even responsible enough to show up for work on time and how he had to take their crap about keeping me up late at night like newlyweds do. I had humiliated him for the last time. "He grabbed me and started shoving me around the bathroom shaking my arms violently and when I started to cry and mentioning to be careful for the baby, he went wild, "I will put an end to that nigger's baby."

He threw me down on the bathroom floor and repeatedly kicked me in the stomach with his steel-toed shoes. I tried hard to cover my stomach but he wasn't going to allow that to happen. He continued to kick and I lay there just staring motionless into his eyes for I felt as good as dead myself, in fact I was dead, I was dead to life, to love, to hopes, and to dreams. At this point nothing mattered in fact just kill me off I thought then there would be no more Nanell to kick around to blame to hate to laugh at.

He left and as I stood up I felt all the cramping and heaviness of the world in the pit of my bottom. Soon a warm rush of bright red, the room spun I felt hot and weak and nauseous. I couldn't even cry I just felt like I was watching a horrible movie of myself in the midst of losing my baby. I lay down on the floor and curled up into the fetal position and hung on to each pain of life that would soon take a life from me. I soon expelled the fetus, the baby of my dreams. Quickly I dripped blood through the bathroom and into the kitchen where I grabbed the paper towels and went into the bathroom silently crying trying to wipe the blood from the floor.

Taking my panties off meant losing the baby from my body, losing the touch of the lifeless baby that had just come from within me. I put my panties into the garbage bag and took the paper towels and picked up the beginning of life that had now ended and put it in the garbage can. I was brought back to reality with the phone ringing and the cafe wondering if I was alright and if I was coming to work as it was Tuesday and on Tuesdays we had to serve fifty for Kiwanis. Quickly I changed uniforms, cleaned the rest of the bathroom, took out the garbage and put my best smile on and went to work. My aching physically and emotionally was buried deep inside of me. I was in that garbage can with my baby, the baby that was taken from me.

Life Goes On and On

I smiled and served my customers in the same fashion that I always had. I knew I was going to have to explain how I lost a baby and all that because the gals at work knew that I was so excited to have this baby. Polly had seen me taking some Midol and wondered what was going on. I told her that I had started spotting and was cramping real bad; she suggested that I get to the doctor as soon as I could as this shouldn't be happening well I knew the doctor would be the last place that I would be allowed to go.

When Gradin came home from work and took his usual feel of my crotch he could feel the pad. He grinned at me and said," I suppose now you killed our baby." I never uttered a word or a breath, at that moment I could have killed him and felt no remorse. That bastard was no damn different than any other man, all men ever do is take from you, screw you, and leave you feeling more empty than the meaning of empty could ever portray. In fact men brought a completely new meaning to the word empty, life taking, and life sucking a-- holes.

Time and life went on, the days rolled into weeks and weeks into months. Soon Gradin desired to move back to Russell to have his own welding business he was tired of working for others. However, we continued to live in Madison and moved into a different house to rent. I don't even remember why we did now. I want to say that Gradin got into a fight with the landlord on the noise coming from our apartment. I am not very sure on that and all I knew was what Gradin would tell me and that sure as hell did not mean that it was the truth.

I had stopped at the welding shop to tell Gradin that I was going up to the Laundromat to do laundry and that is where I would be if he tried to call me and I didn't answer. He came out to make sure that there was dirty laundry in the baskets and that it at least looked like I was going to do laundry. I told him that I didn't feel good and that my side ached. He made mention that I was always complaining about something and that I wasn't going to the doctor.

While at the laundry mat I got to hurting worse, it was such a sharp pain it nearly brought me to my knees. I had all I could do to get the laundry started, I felt like I was going to die. I immediately drove straight up to the clinic and I must have looked as white as I felt as they took me right in, drew blood and he poked around gently on my stomach, on my left side and he informed me that I had to check in right away as he said I was having an appendicitis attack. I told him I had laundry to finish and to tell my husband. He informed me that this could be deadly if I fooled around as it could break and poison me. I left still in very much pain and not knowing how I was going to be able to tell Gradin that I had gone to the doctor when he had told me not to. I hurried with the laundry and stopped back by his work place. I immediately apologized for bothering him again at work but that I had gone to the doctor because I was in so much pain and that I was suppose to check in to the hospital because they were going to do surgery on my appendix. He was furious and informed me that he was not losing any time on me and that I would have to wait until he was off work before he would take me and that I needn't expect him to hang around there and wait for me.

Finally Gradin arrived home from work and told me to get my ass in the car and that I had better not talk about anything I shouldn't up at that place. The staff was nice and checked me in; the doctor was coming down the hallway and was waiting for me to get ready for surgery. Gradin stuck around until it was time for me to go into surgery then he left. I was scared to death that I might die and I was just as scared of needles. I had always been that way. In fact after they had put me to sleep for the surgery they had to wake me up again and do it all over as I went to sleep shaking so bad that there was no way they could do surgery on me. My appendix had ruptured just as they had taken it out of me and I became death fully sick and had to stay in the hospital longer than they first had said. Gradin never came around until it was time for me to be discharged. It was on a Sunday when he showed up and I was ready to leave the hospital. All Gradin was worried about was how much this was going to cost him and I had better not cost him too much.

Once outside the hospital I seen he had borrowed his friends boat again and was ready to go fishing. I was ready to go home and sit down as I wasn't feeling too good and still having a hard time straightening up. Gradin informed me that I was going fishing and that we were getting back to normal around the house. Once out in the boat he started his same picking on me, soon he was gently rocking the boat and I asked him to stop as it was hurting in my incision. Well that was all he needed to hear to do just the opposite, he started rocking the boat harder nearly making the water come in and laughing and laughing I had all I could do to keep from crying. I was in such pain! Finally the bluegills started biting and thank God as it got his mind off rocking the boat.

Soon his conversation turned to sex and how I had better be ready to perform tonight as he had gone long enough without it. I told him I didn't think I could stand to do it tonight as I was still very sore and tender. He informed me that I would be ready to do it when he wanted it. After returning home he brought in the fish and decided to clean them in the kitchen. I couldn't say anything as it was his house and his way. He drank more beer and started getting a mess going in the kitchen. I stayed out of the way until he yelled for me to come in there and get him a bowl and informed me that I could clean up the mess when it was done and to be sure and take the fish heads out wrapped in newspaper. As I looked around the kitchen and watched I could see the fish scales had landed on the counter, the back wall, the cupboard doors, and the ceiling. I just wanted to cry as this was going to be such a mess and long drawn out process to get it all cleaned up and ready for his inspection. I was tired and hurting and just wanted to go to bed but then I knew that was a long ways from happening this night.

It was a little after one in the morning when I finished standing on the cupboard getting the last of the scales off the ceiling. I still had to take the garbage out and wash the kitchen floors and he was sitting in the living room drinking and telling me to hurry up. Finally I had to go in the bathroom and clean myself off and get rid of this ugly day but I could not wash the pain away nor the fear of what yet may happen.

As I slid into bed on my side, my edge of the bed, here he come roughly grabbing my arm and telling me how long it had been and that it had been long enough. I bit my lip and grimmest and shut my eyes, the sting of pain came deep within my incision. Repeating "have mercy on me" over and over in my head. Gradin fell silently on his side of the bed. I lay there listening for his breathing to ease into that of a deep sleep. Quietly I slid out of bed, it hurt to try to stand up and my incision was stinging.

Upon entering the bathroom and adjusting my eyes to the light I could see that some of my top layer stitches had torn, I didn't want to look at the rest of it but I had to. I sat down on the toilet holding my side and crying, crying about the pain, crying over the trap I was in and not being able to figure out my way out. Hell I didn't want out as there was nowhere to go, I just wanted him to love me then everything would be OK. Why did every aspect of life have to hurt? I gently held my skin together and started putting band-aids on it thinking that might hold it together. It looked more than a quarter inch deep and some blood and oozing. The rest of the night I spent on the couch curled up in the fetal position. The tighter I could roll myself up the better I felt. I didn't want to be touched, I only wanted to hold me tight and be alone.

Sleep finally came and with it the ability to escape from the day.

The next beating was over the hospital bill. His insurance had covered it all-all except twelve dollars. The fury in his eyes matched that of a person losing a million dollars and yet this was about twelve dollars.

Moving to Russell

We moved into an apartment above the Laundromat. There were two apartments and we could pick whichever one we wanted. We picked the back apartment so we would not hear the noise out front of the building. There was a living room with a closed door that when that was opened looked into the kitchen of the adjoining apartment. We just kept it locked, and then we had our kitchen and bedroom off the kitchen. The rent was $75.00 a month, Gradin went to work cleaning up his welding shop, I don't remember what kind of terms he made on that or how we paid for that. Maybe his dad helped him I do not know.

They had bingo in Russell one night a week and his mother would pick me up and go. I loved her and I loved playing bingo. One night I actually won a $100. 00, she told me to keep that for myself, and I told her Gradin would never let me. She told me to hide it in my pillowcase and that he would never know. I was so excited; I felt rich and that maybe I could even buy myself a pair of shoes. A pair of shoes that I wanted but never was able to get.

He came home for lunch and it was quiet. Guess that was better than fighting, after he left for work I cleaned up the kitchen and did some unpacking. Around three that afternoon he stopped by home smelling of liquor and wild eyed. He asked me if I won anything at bingo and I told him I had not. With that, he scurried me through the room and threw me on the bed and himself on top of me, with his nose close to mine he asked me again if I was lying and I said no. It was then that he back handed me and told me he heard up town that I had won a hundred dollars. He kept yelling at me and striking me and wanted the money. I cried and was telling him that his own mom told me I should keep it and not tell him. After all it was my money. He just grinned and held out his hand and as I reached it out of the pillowcase he shoved me away and told me to never keep money from him or anything else for that matter and that my money was for him. I did ask if I could please get a pair of new shoes and he lunged at me telling me that I got nothing and do not ask again.

Later that day when his mom stopped by I told her what happened and she said I would not have given it to him. She weighed close to 350 pounds, if I were that size I wouldn't give up anything either but I wasn't that size I was less than 100lbs

Our first Christmas we went out to his parent's house which was filled with laughter, beer, and cheer! His family always had pickled herring to eat at Christmas and Gradin wanted me to try some. I politely said, "No thank you." Before I knew it he straddled me between his legs down on the floor. With a fork in one hand and holding my hands away from my mouth with his other, he packed pickled herring in my mouth and held my mouth shut. The juice from this burned its way up my nostrils and ran down my face. He was so mad at me for putting up a fuss, I was not allowed up until I swallowed the pickled herring.

Russell became our permanent home as we bought a house for $1,500 just north of the bank and near the lake. Gradin made me lie about my age when we signed for the loan. We had driven into Marshall and I remember being parked on the side street off main street and he told me to stay in the car and he went inside, soon he came out and opened my door knelt down by me and informed me I was to lie about my age so we could get this loan. I was too scared to lie and being caught if I did not lie it would be another beating, there was no good outcome in this situation.

We were able to get the home but it was based upon a lie, a lie about my age. Once again, I had the image of happily ever after. All I had to do was keep the home clean enough and learn to be at his disposal and we would be so happy. I spent hours scraping off old wallpaper and smoothing down rough plaster and patching holes in the wall.

The beatings and abuse continued and the reasoning behind them made no sense at all. It was evident that it did not matter what I did or how I did it I was going to be at his mercy and he would deliver me his wrath. He seemed to stay in a state of anger especially when it came to me. I would watch him laugh with his friends and smile and flirt with the girls and yet he could look at me with such hate, I did not understand why he hated me so. I learned to close up and shut down when people did stop over because if I talked to anyone he became furious that I was talking about him or if I tried to share in conversation he made sure to turn on me and make me sound and look stupid.

One Saturday I had worked and cleaned house all day. I had rented the shampooer and cleaned from top to bottom. The place looked and was spotless. All day the roast simmered and the house was filled with the smell of a seasoned pork roast, I was so happy to have my home cleaned and I thought for sure that Gradin would be pleased to have a clean home and a home cooked meal.

The table was all set everything was set out when he came through the door. Slamming the door shut he headed upstairs to wash up, not once making a comment as he walked through the house

We sat down to eat and then I realized that I had forgotten to set the butter out on the table. Now hard butter was something that made him very mad and why had I forgot that, didn't I care about how he wanted his butter! As I passed him the meat my stomach became more knotted up and I somehow new it was going to be bad, I just did not know how bad. He went to spread his butter on his bread, his bread tore, and with that he threw the knife at me cussing me all to hell. He then grabbed my arm and threw me on the kitchen floor in front of the kitchen stove, next came the ketchup bottle squirting all over me and then the hot roast on top of me.

With a swift kick in the side, he yelled at me to clean up this mess I had caused and with that out the door he went. I sat in the middle of the floor not knowing where to start or what to clean first. I wanted to lock the door to protect myself from him but I knew if he came back and found the door locked he would kill me.

I spent the rest of the afternoon cleaning and shampooing the rug once again. I tried to keep my face towards the kitchen door so I did not have to worry about him sneaking in on me while I had the shampoo machine running. Many times he had sneaked up on me and grabbed my hair from behind or wrapped his arm around my neck from behind.

Beating after Beating

The beatings continued. I remember the Halloween that I had gone to Tyler to the laundry mat and my mother showed up to do laundry. She wanted me to come out to the farm to see dad. She had bought me a winter coat she had gotten on sale. I did not have a winter coat, as Gradin did not want me to have one.

I told her that he checked the mileage on the car and that I was only allowed to go to that laundry mat and back. I had to be home and supper on the table by 6:00p. m. As that was house rule. Mom agreed to drive me out to the farm so I could get the winter coat and to see dad, after all, I was not allowed to go visit them or call them and they were not allowed over to our place.

I could not help but feel very nervous about going behind his back and going out to the farm. Oh, how I had missed my dog, it was good to tussle with him outside. It made my day just to hug and kiss him and to get the love he had kept for me.

The new coat was in a bag in the back seat of the car and I did not know how I was going to be able to ever tell him about it or how I got it or if he would even let me keep it. I knew the only way I might possibly be able to talk him into not being mad and letting me keep it would be the next time we made love. Making love had become my bargaining tool to ask if it was OK to get the basics of life, like a new bra, a new pair of nylons and now maybe get to have a winter coat.

I made it home and got supper on the table in time and I had watched through the kitchen window as he had opened the car door and checked on the mileage. He had not noticed the bag in the back seat. I could not swallow as I watched him and wondered if he had spotted it. I was even afraid to exhale and let anything from the inside of me escape me, not even my very own breath.

During supper he informed me that he had invited a few friends over and that I was to clean the house and to make sure that no one had to wait for a beer. Most of all he did not want to catch me talking to others off by myself as he would beat the ever-loving shit out of me if he caught me talking to anyone alone.

By the time the evening events started, I was upstairs putting the clean laundry away and ironing what needed to be ironed when Joann came running upstairs to greet me. I was very horrified that she had come up. Didn't she know that this was a guaranteed beating for me? I hurriedly whispered to her that we had to go down right away as Gradin did not want me alone with anyone.

We took our place at the kitchen table and I greeted others as they arrived and handed them a beer. I was making popcorn and had several bowls around and Johnny Cash was playing in the background. A couple other gals arrived and we went outside to look at the full moon glistening over the lake and admiring how beautiful it was when all of a sudden it dawned on me that I needed to get back into the house. I hurried in to see his glaring eyes staring me down as he asked for another round of beers.

Finally, I could sit down again in the kitchen. Without warning Gradin came storming from the living room into the kitchen. The girls saw him before I did as I was sitting with my back towards the living room from which he came. He jerked up the back of the chair and dumped me on the floor in front of everyone." You son of a bitch you were talking about me again weren't you?" "No." I replied, and I had not said a word about him but rather we took in the beauty of the moon and the glistening water that danced gingerly under the moon.

As I tried to get up and feeling horrible for laying there in front of everyone and having everyone stare at me, Gradin landed punch after punch on my legs and butt and back with his steel toed shoes on. The next thing I knew he picked me up and hurled me through the kitchen doorway and I sailed through the door to the outside. The screen door flew off the hinges as I landed on my left shoulder out in the yard. He continued to kick me repeatedly and telling me he was going to kill me and kill my parents. As I begged him to stop I realized he was not about to stop and no one was about to stop him as they all stood there with beers in their hands looking on.

All of a sudden, I felt a weight on top of me and it was Joann. Joann had thrown herself down on me like a shield and screamed at him to stop hitting me. With that, Gradin turned toward the porch and grabbed two guns and the car keys. Everyone just stood there watching and no one said a word as he threw the guns in the front seat and grabbed bullets from his work truck. He then jumped into the car and spun dirt all the way out of the yard.

Joann helped me back in the house and wondered whom she could call for me so someone could come get me. I did not know what to do so I had her dial his parents after all they lived only 3 miles away. When I got on the phone with Gradin's dad and told him what happened he started to yell at me and tell me I could not come there that us kids had better figure things out.

Again, here I was all alone and nowhere to go and the thought of him out there with two guns and his last words was he was going to kill my parents, and me! I had better get a hold of mom and dad. After getting dad on the phone, I begged him to leave at once and to take mom with him as Gradin had left with two guns and was probably on his way over there as he was going to kill them. I begged dad not to take the normal roads over to get me, as he would no doubt run into Gradin.

Most everyone had left the party but Joann stayed near me and I feared for her too as it was not safe to be anywhere around. Finally, mom and dad showed up and by the time they did I was hurting more and more. I hurt so bad I did not know what area to complain about first. My shins, my shoulder, my butt, and my back were full of bruises.

We seen Joann out so we knew she was safe in the night of hell and dad and I quickly looked around the house. I showed dad where I was in the kitchen and how he threw me out the door and I sailed across the porch and through the screen door. I had sailed at least fifteen feet by the time I landed in the yard.

Death would have been a blessing at this point, as I did not know there were any other options. Dad talked gently to me about going to Ivanhoe to the Sheriff's office and see if they would arrest Gradin or do something. I was not sure about that as I already thought we were all going to die and that it was just a matter of time.

As we entered the sheriff's office Buddy was the sheriff and dad knew him from way back or at least he thought he did, he sure figured Buddy would help us out. Buddy asked me to explain what had happened and wanted to know what I had done to cause this. YES, YOU HEARD ME WHAT HAD I DONE TO CAUSE THIS! Before I could begin he wanted me to know that I could not run home every time I had an argument and that mom and dad now had their own life to live and shouldn't have to worry about me. "Besides, all married couples are going to have squabbles now and then you should know that."

When he asked me or presumed it was the first time I began to unravel like a ball of yarn that had been tightly wound. I told of losing my baby in the light of day and not being able to tell anyone and how I had to go to work and smile as if nothing happened. If you think this is the first time and I caused it then you are wrong and you cannot help me. Gradin is a very mean man and it will not matter what I say here, as he will kill me. "Please could we make sure he is not at the farm with his guns waiting in the grove to kill us?"

Buddy said he could do that but that there was nothing he could do to Gradin as this had happened in Lyon county and not Lincoln county.

As I look back years later with a ton of education under my belt and having survived my past, I think how he, the sheriff, never wrote a report, never took one picture. He gave me a pat on the back and said, "Remember now try not to make him mad and you should be alright." Ya I got that, I got that very well. Thanks for nothing was all I could think. However, I smiled and told him I appreciated his help and thanked him.

As we pulled in the driveway, we could see the deputy's car with his spotlights on checking over the buildings. He appeared to care more and was concerned for our safety and promised to stay close to our farm until it was time for him to get off duty and he would be watching.

He helped me into the house and dad made coffee for everyone. I laid down on the couch in the living room and tried to find a spot that did not hurt. Mom and dad were just off to the side and they left their bedroom door open so we could talk. We had no locks on our door, which the deputy said we should get. Hell we never had to worry about anything out in the country. Tonight we had a lot to worry about.

I strained to stay awake and was staring at the mess of windows we had in the living room, one above my head and one at my feet and one across from the couch. I could not fight the need for sleep and the fight to stay awake and try to stay alive. After falling asleep, I awoke crying and screaming. I thought the house was on fire as the flames flickered on the wall near me. Dad came out and assured me that that son of a bitch was not going to kill me or do a damn thing to any of us. What I was seeing was the shadow of the flames flickering from the front glass of the oil burner.

With the Morning Sun

With the break of the morning sun shining all the way through the house from the kitchen, I awoke to what should have been a beautiful day. I could not lift my head off the pillow. It even hurt to turn my head and I started to cry. Dad came in with fresh coffee and I could not lift my head off the pillow. He helped me up and my shoulder hurt so bad I thought my neck and arm were going to fall off. That heavy feeling made me feel like I was going to tip over.

Dad talked me into going to the emergency room as he felt too that I had probably hurt it quite bad. After having several x-rays done, they discovered that I had a broken collarbone. When I left the hospital, I had a new slug of worries! Where was all the money going to come from to pay for all this! One of my many beatings was having cost him a whole $12.00 that the insurance did not pay after my last surgery.

I had a harness to wear to hold my arm up and take all pressure off the collarbone and I was to wear the harness for six weeks. How could I work or do anything with this stupid thing around my neck.

There had been more mornings than I care to remember, waking up stiff and sore and empty and not knowing what to do. Where do I go, how do I go, as there was no means for me to go. I could not stay here with mom and dad as mom was already pissed about having to help me and run to me in the middle of the night. With my mindset, I thought she was right and I was wrong. After all her and dad were still together after all the years of cheating and drugs and mental illness. Here I am and I cannot even keep a marriage together or make one person happy.

When dad finished chores and came in for breakfast, he sat there as I had seen him so many times before rubbing his fingers in the palm of his other hand biting down on his pipe stem and staring at the floor. I knew he had something on his mind and was about to tell me. The familiar knot was in my stomach, the knot that taken up permanent residence in my stomach these days. After a fashion dad started telling me without looking at me that, he was afraid that Gradin was going to kill me and he thought I should get a lawyer and file for divorce. I cried feeling even more like a failure as I had no money for a divorcee, no job, nowhere to go either.

Dad put in a call to Judge Crump and talked with him for a short period and he had suggested too that I should get an attorney. Well from my shoes that felt as impossible as the chance of winning a million dollars. I just felt lost and all alone. Bottom line is I knew that dad did not have the money and I had no money but aside from that, all I knew deep in my heart was that Gradin would kill me rather than let me leave, after all, I was his property or so he had me believing.

Gradin called and I was scared and I was glad. He was crying so I knew he felt bad and he loved me. He wanted me to come home and I did not know what to do as I knew that dad did not want me to go back and yet I knew that I could not live there with mom and dad nor did I want to. Gradin promised me that never again would he hit me. He never said a word when I told him that he had broke my collarbone. He just wanted to make sure that dad was not going to hurt him when he came to get me and I assured him that he would not do anything.

Gradin showed up, he looked rather sheepish, and yet I had a knot in my stomach, as I knew things would probably not change but maybe this time. He hugged me and told me to get in the car. I slid over by him and we drove off towards home. We were no more than a mile up the road when he told me to move over to stay on my side of the car and then proceeded to tell me that the only reason he came and got me at all was so his mom would talk to him. He ran his fingers along my collarbone harness and started laughing. I looked at him through tear-filled eyes and again he laughed at my swollen shins and puffy lips. It was all a big joke to him and he was not sorry. Oh, why did I fall for it again? All I wanted to do was go home, be his wife, and love him. He did not have to be mean to me at all.

Upon arriving at home, he told me to take my clothes off and lay down. I asked him if we had to as my shoulder hurt and as soon as the words escaped my lips I seen the coldness come over the eyes that not long before that appeared to hold a sheepish look. How could one person's eyes show so much anguish and coldness? I shut my eyes and gritted my teeth and finally it was over. He always left me sore and feeling empty feeling raped feeling less than a human being.

All my baths from childhood on consisted of wanting to scrub the hurt and touch of others off me. What I did not realize is that the mind can never be washed of the memories no soap could take them away and no amount of scrubbing. How does one take the ugliness of others that has entered their body and learn to let the ugly co exist within? What was said and what was put into you was ugly and it is there to stay. How then do I ever feel clean and rid myself of the ugliness?

There was another time I remember the day I got out of the hospital for peptic ulcers. Gradin came, he drove me home. All the way home he had to describe in detail about the pretty blond that he had screwed in our bed. I sat silently and cried and when we pulled into the driveway he looked at me, laughed, and said, "Do you think I really did that?" His laughter was loud and piercing just as piercing as his words. I went upstairs. I wanted to get away from his glare but he followed me up and told me to run his bath water. Our bathtub was in our bedroom with no doors or curtains to close it off from the rest of the room. He made me sit on the bed while he soaked in the tub and told me we were going to

Ghent to the local bar and dance hall. He told me to clean up and try not to look so ugly and fat.

As I started around the bed, I noticed a clump of blond hair on the rug and my heart sank, why he really had another woman here in our bedroom. I looked at him holding the clump of hair up when he grinned at me I seen all I needed to see in those eyes to know that it was true. Every bit if his story was true and he told it to me to hurt me to crush me but most of all to let me know that I did not matter at all in any way shape or form.

The dance was the last place I wanted to go and it was in the cold of January. I asked if I could just stay home but he was not hearing of that. We had a silent ride to Ghent, some of his friends came over to speak, and Gradin right away started running me down and then asking if anyone had seen Barb. Who was Barb I thought, I had never heard of Barb at all. I asked him permission to go to the bathroom and he let me go. I was so scared as I just knew this was going to be a very bad evening. When I returned to the table there he was with a blonde-haired person beside him. Gradin ordered me to bring him and Barb a drink and that I had better hurry and I was to not buy myself anything. I had to serve them with a smile, so there I was bringing drinks to him and this blonde that later I learned was Barb. Barb was the one who had been at my house and slept in my bed with my husband.

They went and danced and I had to sit and watch. Out of the corner of my eye I seen Sheriff Tom at the dance but he was in civilian clothes and dancing. When I noticed Gradin and Barb had gone outside I went over to Tom and told him who I was and that I just knew I was going to get beat that night and that he was with his girlfriend outside and I was scared. Mr. Tom informed he was off duty and that I would have to find my own ride home.

We ended up at a trailer party in Ghent. I did not want to go in but I had to. Gradin told me to keep my mouth shut and do not talk to anyone. He told me he was going to get something to eat but that I could not have any. I was fine with that as my stomach was upset the way it was and my mind danced with visions of what was yet to come when we got home. This time I told myself I would not go back. I was back in reality with a shove to my shoulder as Gradin sat down by me.

I tried to pull my dress down and keep my legs tight together; I wanted to feel myself hugging myself. All of a sudden, Gradin reached over, jerked at my dress, and yelled, "Look how ugly my wife is." He kept trying to pull my dress way up. I resisted a little and then he jerked me towards him, reached under my butt with his hand, and pulled my dress up until he had it up around my waist exposing my panties and nylons. He sat there laughing at me and I kept my head bowed down. Maybe if I did not look at them then maybe they would not really see me.

On the ride home he was driving so, so fast, there were finger drifts across the road, and at times, it was very hard to see. I clutched the door handle wondering if we were going to be in an accident. I could see up ahead that there was a stop sign before turning on the busy highway and I could tell Gradin had not let up off the gas. As gently as I could I pointed out that there was a stop sign ahead. Instantly the brakes came on and "bam" my forehead bounced off the dashboard. My head began to ache and hurt bad, he was yelling at me for criticizing his driving. He then grabbed the back of my hair, slammed my face into the dash again, and made me tell him I was sorry for what I had done.

We arrived home, Gradin went upstairs to the bathroom, and at one point he yelled at me to get my ass in bed and I better be naked. With all my heart, I had hoped that I could have stayed downstairs long enough for him to pass out then I could plan my escape. I undressed and crawled beneath the cold sheets and slid just as close as I could get to my side of the bed. Gripping the rope on the edge of the mattress I kept my head tucked down and pulled my long hair tightly under my neck in hopes that he would not hit me from behind. I did not want to face him either so I laid still in hopes when he did come to bed that he would think I was sleeping.

Out of the bathroom he stumbled across the room, slid part way on the bed, and informed me I had a mess to clean up in the bathroom. When I did not move quickly enough he was on me like a fallen dead weight and he stunk like vomit. With a fist full of my hair, he dragged me off the bed and down the short hall to the bathroom doorway; it was there that he shoved me down on the floor and rubbed my face in his vomit. He pulled me up by my hair, shoved my face up close to the mirror, and told me to take a good look at myself. When I did not open my eyes, he slammed my face against the mirror leaving a puke smudge for my eyes to rest upon. Laughing he said, "This is you this is what you look like. Now clean it up you stupid bitch and do not come to bed until it is shined up." I took my time cleaning the bathroom as I hoped upon hope that he would just pass out.

Once again, the break of dawn finds me yet in another beating and wondering where to go and how to get there. Around six in the morning, I quietly got the keys and went out, started the car, and drove out to his parents who lived like three miles away and pulled in the yard. This time I did not knock on the door but rather walked in and sat at the kitchen table. His dad peaked around the corner and smiled. I just started to cry pointing out the lump on my forehead. Mom D came around the corner about that time and was yelling at Dad that something had to be done with that kid before he killed me.

The abuse was never ending and humiliating. Each time I did leave the fear of him coming after me and killing me, grew greater than the fear of being beat. Anytime I drove to work or to the grocery store, I always watched behind me, as I was sure he would get me and jump me somewhere. The idea of a place being safe for me to go to was never a part of my thoughts.

There was the time that he asked me to change the TV channel and I ask him if he could wait as I was just finishing washing dishes when all of a sudden he came around the corner and grabbed me by my long hair and hurled me at the TV. I landed my shoulder up against the TV, the same shoulder he had already broke. He then shoved my face against the TV screen and shouted for me to change the channel. I then had to wait until he gave me permission to get back up.

Then the next time he might come around the corner and hug me from behind. I kept my body stiff in anticipation for the blow that would eventually come. My house was spotless and you could have eaten off the floor. Nothing was ever left out of place; the ashtrays were even washed.

Beating after beating, set up after set up, there was no winning and if I won then what did I really win? Freedom until what the next beating! The money from my pay checks along with the receipt for groceries and or gas better match up to the pay stub or there was hell to pay. I could get by once and awhile saying I bought a pop but there was no way to really gain any money for escaping, besides he had told me a long time ago that the car was in his name and that he would get me for stealing if I decided to take off.

My life was nothing more than that of a beaten dog. You see if you put a dog in a cage and every time it tries to come out and you hit the dog, eventually you can leave the door to the cage open and the dog will not leave because he knows what happens. I found my live to compare to that of a dog. There were no new clothes; I was given the bare minimum in order to survive. When we went on a trip to Missouri to see his sister I was not allowed to eat or drink on the way down, as he did not want to have to take time to stop. If I needed the bathroom, he would not stop unless he had to go. It was nothing for him to eat and drink in front of me and grin at me the whole time he did this. I did not dare complain. I had no voice, I had no legs to walk away, and I had no money, no vehicle. Who would help me, who could I trust?

When I finally did leave him, I had sixty-eight cents to my name. I moved in with some girls that asked me to leave within less than a week, as they were scared of Gradin driving by the house, calling, and threatening me. I slept in a cornfield approach backed in out of site with all my belongings in a single laundry basket. I fought sleep because of the corn stalk rustling I just knew it was him hiding there and watching me. I would wash up at work at BH Electronics where Toby Smith was my boss. He was very kind and he knew I was taking beatings. I felt half-starved; frightened to death to leave work for fear he would be waiting for me.

With Toby's suggestion to seek counseling, he referred me to one he knew. Mrs. Letty I had known her from Madison when she worked in the basement of the hotel as a counselor there. I had brought her coffee and rolls and hated to see her leave. Now I was referred to her. First though, I had to call in to her office and give all my information over the phone to the secretary about my life, the beatings, and names of course. Upon arrival I completed the small details she needed and then she led me back to a room, she no sooner shut the door then she opened it again. She introduced herself to me as Betty, Barb's mom. Barb was the girlfriend that Gradin made me buy drinks for and the girlfriend that he brought home and I had to cook their meal and serve them. Barb was the one he wanted to screw first and then me. I could not believe my ears this too had to be a set up. She told me to think about talking to her daughter to help her daughter see that Gradin was not a good person. What more could be asked of me? How could I help a fifteen-year-old gal when I could not help myself at the age of twenty? By the time Mrs. Letty came in, I sat silently and cried and she asked how she could help me. How could she help me? How could I trust talking to her without her secretary seeing my folder and my comments and my heartache? I cried and cried and finally I told Mrs. Letty about her secretary and she assured me she would talk to her and that my file would be kept in her safe in her office and only for her eyes. She asked me what I wanted and I told her I wanted to build a wall so high that no one ever gets in again to hurt me. I do not want to feel anything and I do not want anyone to touch me.

She thought I should go to college and take some courses. Ha, I had nowhere to live; no money for college and

I was too retarded for school that I knew for sure. Where was this woman coming from? Did she not hear my trail of survival only I did not see it as survival but a way of life and a life that I did not appreciate or love. I hated my very existence, as I knew not why I existed. Am I still by brother's keeper, am I required to reach out to Gradin's girlfriend? My main concern was leaving that building and not finding Gradin in the parking lot. My boss agreed to cover for me if he should call there for me and he kept me on the clock, as he knew I would be beat for taking time off. I had to hope that Barb did not tell Gradin that her mom seen me and where and why.

Twenty-One But Much Older

After the divorce I was allowed to remain at the house until it sold. I was married for three years and divorced by age twenty one. On my twenty first birthday his parents wanted to take me out to eat and they did not care what Gradin said as he was done with me. After our meal and visiting they brought me back to the house. There in the screen door was a gift for me, as I held the gift and walked through the door into the entryway, the street light lit the entry up so there was no need to turn the light on. By the door was another birthday present and as I reached down to get it I seen the door to the kitchen was setting ajar. I knew that I had locked the door on my way out. That knot in the pit of my stomach began to take over my fears. I was certain that he was inside the house. As I walked through the house I crouched down in fear just sure that he was going to hit me from behind. A search of the house revealed that he was not there.

That night I slept in the closet which was closer to the doorway than the bed. If he came in I would have a few steps jump on him to get out of the bedroom. Finally sleep came upon me and all of a sudden I was awakened to the sound of a gun and the tinkle of glass breaking. I could not move out of the closet as I was frozen in that spot thinking that life as I knew it would surely end any minute.

In the morning I found a twenty two bullet lodged in the head board of the bed. Pieces of glass lay in the sill and on the floor. Quietly I eased my way downstairs to see what might be waiting for me. In the entry way I found where he had disconnected the wire to the light switch and taped the wires over the top of the switch. I should have been dead. If I would have reached to turn the light on I would have been dead. He did not want me but he did not want anyone else to have me either. I did not want anyone else either as I knew that men will hurt you and use you.

In time, my mother learned I was seeing Mrs. Letty so she started in on me that I must have told her what a bad mother she had been and what did I tell her? The next time I seen mom she gloated to me that she was a new client of Mrs. Letty. It was at that point that I ended my sessions with her. I knew mom would twist and turn stuff like she always did. Maybe mom was afraid how I might have told her that on mom's fiftieth birthday I had a beautiful cake made with a red rose on top and had called the neighbor ladies over to surprise mom for her birthday. When mom got home she came in and said hello with a fake smile then asked me to come out to the car and help her get something. As soon as we were out of ear shot she asked me just what in the sam hell was I doing? I told her I had wanted to surprise her for her birthday and she informed me I better get it ended soon as she was going out with her buddy from Ivanhoe. It was more important for her to run the bars than to have a nice party of coffee and cake. She could cut you like slicing butter with a hot knife. I had also felt that maybe by giving her a party she would stay home. No, mom had fooled the smartest and the dumbest with her crazy ways. Mrs. Letty was swept into mom's circle of friends for what reason I do not know but the day my dad died mom wanted me to call her and tell her so she could come out. I called her in front of mom and Mrs. Letty never came out. She told me to give mom her sympathy and I did. Mrs. Letty later wrote a card and said that she had become too close to mom and had crossed the line and could no longer continue to see her. I think Mrs. Letty, deep down, knew how crazy mom was and she probably did not think she could deal with her craziness. Mom could win the world over and gain self-pity but once it stopped, she was in a shamble. She needed to suck the life out of others in order to have a life.

When my only niece died she never bothered to tell me that she had died. I loved that little girl as she was an angel sent from God. I had taken care of her when her other grandmother died of cancer. I had a special painting done of her and her mother and gave to them. When I could I gave her baby blankets and gifts. Mom drove her wedge in that relationship and once again I was the worthless one but that is alright. God knows what I did and what I said and I sleep good at night. I have since visited her grave and I have the memory of her laughter and touch. My mother informed me after she dropped me out of the will that she was leaving everything for my niece and her mother. I walked away as I never wanted her money. The alone feelings I had were very hard to overcome and not understanding why all this happened. I had defended the little girl's mother against my own brother but that did not mean anything. When mom scattered her seeds of hatred for me and watered the surface with money a lot of things grew and grew against me. When one goes through such mental abuse from their own mother it is hard to overcome but I have with the help of loved ones, counselors, and ministers helping find love and understanding and making me realize that God never once stated that I had to take the abuse of my parents in order to be loved by God.

In time I ended up walking away from my mother but not before she had a stroke and I spent thirty six hours with her. This too ended in heartache and more rejection. She had always told me that she told her Dr. Mudd how I had treated her. How in the hell had I treated her? I cleaned for her, I cooked for her, I helped bathe her, I tried to be there the best that I knew how. I was called out of the hospital room to take a phone call in the lobby from Dave, my brother. He was calling to see if he should come home or if mom was faking it. I told him that the next seventy two hours were going to be critical until they knew that the blood clot had dissolved. I told him he would have to make that decision as I could not make it for him. I also told him I felt she was acting more like she had a nervous breakdown as I had seen plenty of them. We finished our call and I headed down to her room. My husband and Dr. Mudd was standing at the foot of her bed. I smiled as I entered the room and Dr. Mudd said "I don't know what you said to her but you are not allowed in here anymore. I want you to leave immediately." I did not have a damn clue what the hell that was all about and furthermore my husband did not say a word. Not one word was said in my defense. I left in tears and had more anger for Dr. Mudd then I had before this encounter. That all alone feeling with no one standing up for you or helping you, that is what hurt so much. We stayed at her apartment and waited for Dave as we were going to leave in the morning. Dave finally got there and he laughed and yelled, "Hell she has always been crazy you know that." "Why did you give her this picture with this saying about being a wonderful mom, she has never been a mom let alone wonderful." "I do that shit sis because she eats it up." I could never do that because it is not true. "Do you know how hard it is to buy her a card for any occasion because they do not say what a wonderful mom you were by not protecting me and loving me?"

The next morning we did ask permission just to tell her goodbye and the nurses knew how mom was and how Dr. Mudd was so they said go ahead. I rubbed her toe buried under the sheet and said, "Mom we are going to leave now and I hope that you get better. Just be sure to do what they tell you." She looked at me with those coy eyes. "Aren't you even going to kiss me goodbye?" I had not been able to kiss her since I was a child. I told her I wished her well and about that time she bolted up in bed and said, "I'll fix you, you son of a bitch. You are cut out of the will, you will get nothing." Again my husband said nothing and Dave didn't either. I walked out and cried all the way home. I never called her again or bothered her, if she did not want to be my mother then that was fine. She never knew me! I wanted nothing more than to be loved. I did not want her money.

Finally she wrote, sent a Christmas card. Oh that should just fix everything up, a Christmas card for fifty cents was going to wash away the truth, her last sentence to me. I immediately put the postal sticker of return to sender on it. That was a privilege I had as postmaster. On Christmas Eve day I received a letter from Dr. Mudd telling me that in his then fifty four years of living he had dealt with murderers, robbers and rapist and I by far was the worst human being on the planet earth. In church that night for Christmas Eve services I again sat feeling so empty and all alone. My husband sat next to me then the children. Tears streamed down my face through the entire service. He could not even say that was wrong of Dr. Mudd to do that, he could not even say that I was not the worst human being on the planet earth. This letter that is now engraved in my head nearly brought me to an end, my end.

If this were to happen today, I would without a doubt turn him in to the American Medical Association for his being unprofessional. That is today but not then. I to this day do not know what set mom off in between me leaving her hospital bed to take that phone call and returning. It is OK; I do not need to know as God knows. The lesson I walked away on this is, just because someone has a title does not mean that they are educated or know how to handle a situation. Do not be fooled by titles or the lack there of. Dr Mudd never slept under my bed, walked in my shoes or dodged the verbal abuse so who is he to say anything? He is no one and will remain as a no one for the rest of my life. Again God will judge this man that so quickly judged me.

I may have survived all the abuse but not without cost. Later after joining the army, I met my second husband who in turn was an alcoholic cop. From this marriage three children were born. After eighteen years of marriage this too ended in a haze of anger and threatened harm and him being suicidal and drunk in the garage of our home.

The kids all left me in the three-year divorce proceedings for one reason or another but mainly for being confused teenagers and seeing where the freedom lay. My heart continued to break with each of them leaving as I loved them so, they were the one thing I had done right in life and I still had failed them.

When the children were little I ended up going to college and pursing a degree in sociology and a minor in psychology. For me personally it was chapter and verse of what I had grown up in and what I had survived. Learning what the odds were that I had any chance of a normal life was like only three percent. I cried from within, I hated the books that seemed to be a reflection of my weak choices and learning my lack of knowledge in basic math, grammar, and other courses. I knew I was retarded and hated having to go to a higher learning arena, there was no arena or platform for what I had learned in life.

Each course had its struggles right down to volleyball. I never could do the volleyball and almost dropped out of school knowing that was the only course I needed. For me to be down on the playing field and everyone kicking the crap at each others legs brought me back to the steel toed shoes that Gradin wore and had kicked me with so many times. This is not a sport; this only is legalized beatings on the legs. Finally, I had to go talk to the instructor and he actually listened and could see where that would bother me. From that day on until the end of the course I only, need to attend and take notes and write him a paper on volleyball at the end of the semester.

In the end, I graduated with a Bachelor of Arts in Sociology with a three point five grade point average. I left high school with no passing grades from fifth grade on but they pushed me through anyway after all what do you do with the daughter of a crazy lady and a dirt-poor farmer? There would not be much hope held out for anyone in that environment!

What I had grown up in I had survived but I did not do very well, because of what I had lived in. The choices I made in a spouse were bad ones and not just once but three times. All were alcoholics, abusive in their own right. The effects go much deeper than that as the effects of my bad choices have left my children in peril. Both my son's are alcoholics, have been abusive towards others and my daughter, after surviving cancer, made bad choices in her spouse. I refuse to be guilt driven but rather be driven by my guilt. My children know all that I have been through, I have laid out the tools, and it is up to them and only them to make the right choices. I will not allow them to use their living conditions as an excuse for their behavior.

While I did stick it out with their father for eighteen years was I wrong in leaving at all or should I have left years earlier? I have reflected on this question many times. I sometimes think that no man is your friend but every man is your teacher.

The father of my children was a hard core alcoholic cop. I know now that while I did love him, I married him for protection. I just figured if he wore a badge then he would take care of me. I could not have been more wrong.

By the time I was pregnant with our third child I wanted to leave as he was drinking more and more and yet I had no place to go. My mother thought he was everything good and she had already told me that if this marriage did not work then she would know for sure that it was my fault for failing Gradin and now this husband. She asked him why I filed for divorcee when I eventually did and he told her he really did not know why. My daughter knew exactly why. He never brought himself to tell my mother that he had barricaded himself in the garage with a case of beer and a .357. He never told her that he was forced to go into treatment because the cops were very much aware of his drinking problem.

My mother bought him and his new wife a wedding gift. I guess they visited back and forth, that is until he got caught drunk on duty by a state trooper that stopped to help him with his arrest of a DUI. During the arrest the trooper smelled booze on him and hauled him off to treatment. When he was allowed to come back on duty, it was stated in the minutes of the city meeting, he would have to take a breath test before and after work. On his death bed from brain cancer he told my daughter that if he got to feeling better he was going to go on the biggest drunk ever!

A House with No Foundation

As with any foundation, a portion is buried in the ground and the rest stands to the elements of time, the elements of man. The child within me lay beneath the surface gently out of sight and seen only by me. As for what is left standing is the voice of the silent, the voice for those who have died at the hands of others.

God spoke to me one evening as I was driving over to a speaking engagement in from of the FHA. Their teacher had heard about me and asked me to come and speak. As the music played on the radio my mind raced with why are you doing this, will they understand, will they be kind? All of a sudden, the news came on and a lady had died at the Sioux Falls SD. Hospital after having lain for five days from the beating her husband gave her. God gave me life and he gave me a voice. A voice to share, to teach, to reach out to others, to be a beacon of light for those yet in the dark.

Tell

The following statement is found and documented at the concentration camp of Dachau. "Tell what they did to us". It was their code, their desire to survive and tell the world what happened. This statement screamed so loudly in the silence of my night to tell what they did to me only it was not by Hitler but by the ones that were to love me.

My courage to tell is finally free. My embedded fears of all my yesterdays rushed at the child within, and cried out for the last time to be nurtured like I had never been before.

Courage can never be measured in a cup or held in your hands. A simple unseen grain of courage can bring down the biggest and the best and a grain of courage can make a mountain out of a pebble. The easiest road to travel is the road that is most traveled; there in itself lies ones biggest challenge. I may never know exactly where it is that I am headed, but I damn sure know where it is I shall never go again.

I struggle to leave the correct message for my children as well as others that feel lost or abandon. It is with this thought in mind I believe like this: What is the magic potion I could give so that you could squeeze so much happiness and living out of a life time that offers so much imitation to living. Clear your path, build your road, and drink from your cup of internal knowledge, wisdom, and insight. Be not blinded by half-truths and hidden agendas. There will be days when you and you alone are the only one that believes in you so be worth believing in. Now this was a big one for me because I thought I was nothing because of what others had done to me. Frankly, no one ever told me I was anything, or worth anything, or loved, or needed. Most of my youth was spent surviving, feeling like a freak, made from the leftovers of God's mixing bowl. Nothing more than a patch quilt of life's experiences. Knowledge, courage, and wisdom will be yours when you learn to "hold on" one minute past the time everyone else would have given up. Yes, I have been there by the hands of others and by my own hands. You know you are alone when you realize you could have killed yourself and no one would have missed you or come to look for you. It is at that moment of exposed pain when the naked fiber of hope seems all gone; it is then that you hang on still not knowing why. When you break down and hold yourself as you wish someone else would have held you

I sat on the couch with my. 38 in hand leaning over the fire place platform on the floor holding the gun to my head and figuring if I leaned just right off the couch I could land on the platform and that way I would not create a big mess. Maybe the carpet would even be OK. One thing for sure, I wanted to end my pain as nothing seemed real or mattered, after all if those that are in charge of my growing years did not give a damn about me then why should I? I do not want to live to only be hurt and abused more. Why is it so hard for someone to love me, to see me, to hold me? What is a loving touch, a touch without motive? Come on you want a piece of me well if I kill myself then you all lose and be damned this life of pain.

You can't tell me it will be OK or that it will end when you have not seen through my eyes and you have not felt what my heart has felt. You have not had titled people put you down, scorn your very existence and a mother to tell you that you are the one lie your dad told. Who then is in my presence to say you are worthwhile? No one! No one! No one!" The phone rings and it is my friend Edith, "What you up to" "I want to kill myself and I am sitting here with my gun wanting to end it all. No one needs me, I am not good for anything and I can't take it anymore. No one understands." "I understand, please do not do this. I need

143

you, I care. I know you hurt." She was crying she really cared. "I do not want to get that call that you are dead, please do not do that to me."

At the very instant of breaking, you begin to build. The mere single strand of thirst and hunger for life, for your life, is the very basis to build upon. At this moment, you become wiser to the world in which you live. The sheer knowledge of what could have been in your darkest moment plunges at the depth of your soul; it is then that your blindness becomes your light.

Acceptance is also a much-needed quality to have and to enhance. Accepting our limitations does not necessarily mean we have a lack of faith or that we have failed. It does not mean we have given up our confidence in God's omnipotence, goodness, or desire to make us healthy and whole. Instead, we are deciding to trust God in the midst of an undesirable situation.

This I Believe

Henry Van Dyke once said," Remember that what you possess in this world will be found at the day of your death to belong to someone else, but what you are will be yours forever."

My pain and suffering is not mine alone. I am well aware that there are others that suffered far worse than I did. Do not be afraid to leave an abusive situation. Be wise about leaving, make a plan, solicit a friend if you have one. Your weakest moment can and will become your strongest moment. A moment will be just that a moment in time. Your life can change and will change but that is alright as it is good to grow and to develop and find out who you are what you like and what you need. The greatest gift you can give yourself is independence and the ability to survive on your own. It is a lesson and thought process that will get you through life.

Am I always happy? No! Am I perfect? No far from it! Am I free to be me? Yes, I am and I will never give that up again or give it away to anyone. I am free in God's love and cradled within His arms. I know too that we are only as sick as the secrets inside of us. I was very sick at one time as I had many secrets; I have healed and continue to heal.

I have grieved the loss of a baby taken from me in the mid morning sun and I have grieved the loss of myself as a child. The person that was born in me died in me. I cannot go back nor do I want to go back. Therefore, I have let go and have learned a new way of life. Sorrow and sadness have been filed under the past and only used now to teach, to share, to make others think.

Be careful how you judge and why you judge. You too have baggage. Are you willing to share your baggage with someone? Tread lightly on my soul for it has been pierced many times. This was not easy to write, as it was a journey back into pain, and hell, and darkness and suffering it all over again in hopes of getting it on paper for others to understand. You see you cannot understand what you have not experienced.

For those of you that have struggled with abuse or have experienced abuse, there are no black birds. You are not a black bird. You are a yellow bird and just as beautiful as the birds you have not met yet. You are worthwhile and worthy of love and kindness. Let no one judge you be it doctor, policeman, minister. No one can judge you as no one knows you, no one but God.

Remember too that there is not one doctor out there that has the right to tell you that you are the worst human being on the planet earth. . Every counselor and every minister that I shared that with, along with other professionals, could not believe the lack of professionalism that Dr Mudd displayed. I know now that I had every right to walk away and I am glad that I did.